Managing Performance in the Public Sector

Performance thinking has a substantial impact on the management of public organizations, as governments around the world use performance measurement to evaluate their products and services. But as indicators of success, how effective are these systems? And how do these measuring tools impact on our society?

Managing Performance in the Public Sector deals with these questions and offers an important critique of these evaluation systems. In an analysis of the pros, cons, risks and limitations of these systems the author argues that, instead of maximizing performance benefits, they often just create bureaucracy, stem innovation and damage professionalism. Taking a bold stance in a contentious debate, this book presents several strategies for turning performance measurement into a useful instrument that can benefit both students and professionals. An informed analysis of the arena, this is an essential text for anyone studying performance management in the public sector.

Hans de Bruijn is Professor of Organization and Management at the Department of Policy, Organization and Management, Delft University of Technology, The Netherlands. He has wide experience as a reseacher and adviser to public agencies and has conducted extensive research in public management.

Managing Performance in the Public Sector

Hans de Bruijn

Routledge
Taylor & Francis Group

LONDON AND NEW YORK

First published in Dutch in 2001
as *Prestatiemeting in de publieke sector*
by Lemma Publishers

English language version published 2002
by Routledge, an imprint of Taylor & Francis
11 New Fetter Lane, London EC4P 4EE

Simultaneously published in the USA and Canada
by Routledge
29 West 35th Street, New York, NY 10001

Routledge is an imprint of the Taylor & Francis Group

© 2002 Hans de Bruijn

Typeset in Times by Exe Valley Dataset, Exeter
Printed and bound in Great Britain by
TJ International Ltd, Padstow, Cornwall

British Library Cataloguing in Publication Data
A catalogue record for this book is available from the British Library

Library of Congress Cataloging in Publication Data
A catalog record for this book has been requested

ISBN 0-415-30037-1 (hbk)
ISBN 0-415-30038-x (pbk)

Contents

Illustrations

Acknowledgement

Translated and published with permission from *Prestatiemeting in de publieke sector*, copyright 2001 by Lemma Publishers. All rights reserved. Lemma Publishers is not responsible for the accuracy or quality of the translation.

Acknowledgment

Part I

1 An introduction to performance measurement

The beneficial effect of performance measurement

1 Introduction and outline of the argument in this book

In recent years, management techniques from industry have penetrated deep into public organizations. It is felt that, like companies, authorities provide products and services and that their performance can be appraised. A court can be appraised by standards such as the number of judgments it passes, a police force by the number of fixed penalty notices it issues and scientists by the number of their publications in scientific journals. A government organization that manages to define its products can show its performance, which may improve the effectiveness, efficiency and legitimacy of government action.[1]

1.1 A fruitless debate: public profession versus accountability

It is remarkable that positions are easily taken in the debate about performance measurement in the public sector. On the one hand there is the view that performance measurement does not do any justice to the nature of the activities performed by public organizations. Public organizations are professional organizations providing public services. These public services are multiple (they must do justice to different values) and are rendered in co-production (in cooperation with third parties). A school must make its pupils perform well, but also have a good educational climate; its pupils' performance depends on the school's effort, but also on the extent to which pupils are stimulated at home. A court must pass judgment as soon as possible, but its judgment must be well-considered; a court can hardly influence the number of cases it must deal with and the behaviour of the litigating parties. Performance measurement reduces this complexity to one single dimension.

A director who imposes production targets on a professional organization and is later pleased to find that they have been achieved is fooling himself. The example of the Soviet Union's centrally planned economy is often cited. Command a factory to make as many nails as possible from a given quantity of steel, and it will indeed produce many, lightweight, nails. Command the same factory to produce a certain weight in nails, given a certain quantity of steel, and the nails will be made as heavy as possible. In such a system the professional question whether the nails produced are functional is never asked. Something similar applies to public organizations. In many cases it may not be difficult to achieve a certain production, as long as an organization is prepared to ignore professional considerations. Achieving production targets does not tell us anything about the professionalism and/or quality of the performance; an effort to reach production targets may even harm professionalism and quality.

The opposite view begins with the idea of accountability. The more complex the services that public organizations must provide, the more necessary it is to place these organizations at a distance and to grant them autonomy in producing such services. Whilst they are autonomous, they are also accountable, however: how do they spend public funds? Does society receive 'value for money'? After all, granting autonomy to a professional organization may cause it to develop an internal orientation, to be insufficiently client-oriented, to develop excessive bureaucracy and therefore to underperform. Autonomy without accountability conceals both good and bad performance. Lessons can moreover be learnt from accounting for one's performance – be it good or bad.

Accountability is a form of communication and requires the information that professional organizations have available to be reduced and aggregated. Performance measurement is a very powerful communication tool: it reduces the complex performance of a professional organization to its essence. It thus makes it possible to detect poor performance, allowing an organization to be re-adjusted if it performs poorly. Performance measurement can thus also play an important role in acquiring legitimacy for government action.

Both lines of reasoning are rooted in the same development: the need to grant autonomy to professionals performing complex public tasks. This development implies on the one hand that professionals account for their performance: autonomy and accountability go hand in hand. On the other hand, this development implies that it is becoming increasingly difficult to define performance, since autonomy is necessary because the performance is so complex.

This shows that the antithesis set out above is fruitless: both lines of reasoning are correct. An important guideline for the argument in this book is therefore the question whether it is possible to design performance measurement so as to do justice to the complexity of the profession as well as to the need for accountability and, consequently, steering.

Incidentally, professional autonomy is nothing new, of course, for public organizations of a traditionally professional character (universities, the judiciary and the prosecution service). What is new is that these organizations, too, increasingly face accountability.

1.2 An outline of the argument in this book

I intend to make the differentiation referred to above in this book by means of an argument that will proceed as follows.

- First I shall indicate that performance measurement can have a beneficial effect on public organizations. It may improve the professionalism of the service rendered, the public organization's innovative power and the quality of (political) policy making. Appraisals about performance measurement tend to be passed too soon; performance measurement is a much more differentiated activity than is often suggested (this chapter).
- Strong criticism may be levelled against performance measurement. Performance measurement has a great many perverse effects: it may bureaucratize an organization, killing all incentives for professionalism and innovation and causing performance measurement to lead mainly to strategic behaviour. Performance measurement may considerably widen the gap between political policy making and implementation (Chapter 2).
- Many a system of performance measurement sees this development from beneficial effect to perverse effect. I shall then show how the perverse effects will come to dominate the beneficial effects in the long term. This causes systems of performance measurement to lose their effect at some stage, although being very resistant. They survive, even though they have more perverse effects than beneficial ones (Chapter 3).
- This gives rise to an ambiguous picture: apart from the beneficial effects of performance measurement, there are perverse effects. This raises the question how performance measurement can be designed so as to minimize the perverse effects. For this purpose I shall introduce three criteria in Chapter 4 that performance measurement should meet if it is to fulfil its function properly.

These criteria can be used to design a system of performance measurement. This is why I shall refer to them as 'design principles'. I shall work out these design principles in Chapters 5 to 7.

- Chapter 5 will focus on the question how performance measurement can be *trustful*. This means that both management and professionals have confidence in a system of performance measurement. The answer is that a system of performance measurement should be developed in *interaction* between management and professionals. Applying performance measurement also requires such cooperation.

- Chapter 6 deals with *rich* performance measurement. For management as well as for professionals, performance measurement should do justice to the multiplicity of professional activity and not degenerate into a single activity. This is why performance measurement should always tolerate *variety* (in product definitions, for example, or performance indicators, interpretations of production targets).

- Closely associated with this is the idea of *lively* performance measurement. Performance measurement must be an activity that causes management and professionals to feel challenged. I shall set out in Chapter 7 that this liveliness can only be created if performance measurement focuses not only on professionals' products, but also on the process of generating them. Apart from product measurement there is *process measurement*. Liveliness also requires a system of performance measurement to be *dynamic*: it should adapt itself to changing conditions.

- Finally, I shall give an opinion in Chapter 8 about the meaning that performance measurement may have in public organizations.

1.3 Focus and terminology

Performance measurement is used in many organizations. In this book I will deal mainly with public professional organizations. Examples of these may be conventional professional organizations like hospitals, universities and the court service, but also many 'street-level' organizations like the police, the probation service and a large number of departmental implementing bodies.

For the sake of readability, I shall consistently use the terms 'management' or 'director/management' and 'professional/professionals' in this book. The professional is the person who designs the primary process, the director is the person who, by performance measurement among other methods, tries to steer this process and is responsible for it in most cases. This relationship may manifest itself on all sorts of levels in and between organizations. The neighbourhood teams in a police organization (the professionals) are steered by a commander, performing the role of director. In the force command–divisions relationship, these divisions (including their commanders) are the professional units and force command performs the role of director. From a national perspective, the Minister of Justice is the director and the forces are the professional units. In short, the director–professional relationship manifests itself in accordance with this 'Droste' effect on several levels in an organization. The argument in this book may be applied to each of these levels.

In this chapter I shall first give a brief description of performance measurement (Section 2). I shall then discuss the positive effects of performance measurement (Sections 3–5). Next, I shall deal with a number of objections to performance measurement (Section 6) and I shall set out what suggestions there are in the literature to deal with these objections (Section 7).

2 Performance measurement: what it is and its functions

In this section I shall set out – very briefly – how performance measurement is defined in the literature and what functions it may have. For more detailed considerations of these introductory questions I refer the reader to the literature.[2]

The central idea behind performance measurement is a simple one: a public organization formulates its envisaged performance and indicates how this performance may be measured by defining performance indicators. After the organization has performed its efforts, it may be shown whether the envisaged performance was achieved and what the cost of it was.

The problem here is, of course, that the effects of interventions by an authority are often difficult to measure. This is because public performance is multiple and is achieved in co-production. Furthermore, the period between an intervention and its eventual effect may be long. This makes it impossible in many cases to measure the final effect of an intervention by an authority (the 'outcome'), not least when abstract goals such as liveability, safety, integration or quality are involved. What is measurable is the direct effects of interventions by an authority (the 'output': the licence issued, the fixed penalty notice, the article published), while, in some cases – somewhere between direct effects and final effects – intermediate effects might be identified, which are also measurable. Various terms are used for the various effects that may occur in the spectrum between directly measurable and non-measurable: output – outcome; direct effects –

intermediate effects – final effects; output – programme outcome – policy outcome.

It should be pointed out that the terminology in the literature is not always unambiguous. Some writers give the concept 'output' a very narrow definition (only the direct effects), others use a very broad one (including the outcome).[3] In this book I shall confine the meaning of performance measurement to the effects of government action that are measurable. This choice would seem legitimate to me, because it matches much of the everyday language used in organizations: many organizations using performance measurement count the products they generate.[4] Concepts like 'output' or 'product measurement' can be regarded as synonymous with performance measurement; I will, however, widen the concept of performance measurement in chapter 7 by drawing attention to process measurement as well.

Once an authority has defined its products, it can plan the volume of its production over a certain period and establish at the end of this period what production was achieved. As a result, a public organization – like many organizations in the private sector – may pass through a planning cycle, in which performance is planned, achieved and measured. This is often accompanied by a strong orientation on goals. Performance measurement forces an organization to formulate targets for the various programmes for which it is responsible and state the period within which they must be achieved. It will then show its ambitions for each of these targets in performance indicators.

Performance measurement can then fulfil a number of functions.[5] Those mentioned most frequently are the following:

- *Transparency.* Performance measurement leads to transparency and can thus play a role in accountability processes. An organization can make clear what products it provides and – by means of an input–output analysis – what costs are involved.
- *Learning.* An organization takes a step further when it uses performance measurement to learn. Thanks to the transparency created, an organization can learn what it does well and where improvements are possible.
- *Appraising.* A performance-based appraisal can now be given (by the management of the organization, by third parties) about an organization's performance.
- *Sanctions.* Finally, appraisal may be followed by a positive sanction when performance is good or by a negative sanction, when performance is insufficient. The sanction is likely to be a financial one.

These functions have a rising degree of compulsion. Each of these functions can apply to an organization, but also enable comparison – a 'benchmark' – between organizations.

The beneficial effect of performance measurement

In the literature, a great deal of research is available about performance measurement. A first impression – which I shall elaborate on in Chapter 2 – is that performance measurement has a beneficial effect.

3 Performance measurement leads to transparency and is thus an incentive for innovation

First, performance measurement leads to transparency (the above-mentioned function of performance measurement). This transparency is a value in itself. A public organization has limited external incentives for effectiveness and efficiency and therefore also has an almost natural tendency to develop 'red tape': dysfunctional procedures, consultations, structures, etc. This has been beautifully formulated in Parkinson's Law: an increase in employees leads to a reinforced increase in loss of time because internal, non-productive tasks become more voluminous.[6]

The result of this may be that for many activities in an organization it is unclear what they contribute to the primary process and thus to the organization's right of existence. For such an organization to formulate its products and then to meet its performance targets creates transparency, which is an incentive for innovation in the organization. An internal discussion may be started, for example, about how much the various activities contribute to the organization's performance. There is also a clear standard for appraising new procedures or structures: how much do they contribute to the improvement of the organization's performance.[7]

This argument of transparency plays an important role in the United States because it is linked to involving the public ('communities') in the services rendered by authorities.[8] Citizens are invited to define – in consultation with the authorities concerned – services for health care, for example, to formulate goals, to develop performance indicators and to measure performance and publicize it. All this is an incentive for the quality of health care. Transparency here means that agreed goals are made public, which reinforces the incentive.[9] Furthermore, such consultation contributes to authority and citizens feeling jointly responsible for public services rendered.

This is important, since health care performance also depends on the behaviour of citizens.

"What gets measured, gets done'[10] is the summary of arguments of this type: when an organization can make its performance visible, it has goals to concentrate on, and this visibility is likely to be an automatic incentive to improve its performance.

4 Performance measurement rewards performance, prevents bureaucracy

A second cluster of arguments is based on a contrary reasoning: performance measurement is a form of output steering and is desirable, because input and throughput steering are a 'disincentive' for performance.

Input steering particularly rewards the planning and formulating of goals and intentions. It is often an incentive to formulate goals and intentions as ambitious as possible, since one organization distinguishes itself from another by being ambitious. There is also a matching form of strategic behaviour: find out what the director's interests and preferences are and formulate goals in such a way that they match these interests and preferences. The more complex an organization, the more problematic input steering. Complexity means that the relation between plan and implementation is not a matter of course at all; input steering widens this gap because it primarily rewards ambitions (those to the director's liking) and concentrates less on their realization.

'Throughput' steering concentrates on the processes and activities within an organization and not on their results. Here, too, this is no problem in a simple organization, because there will often be a direct connection between an organization's internal activities and its results. In a complex organization the connection between throughput and result is less easy to establish.

Throughput steering, the argument goes, is an 'incentive' for internal activities and a 'disincentive' for performance. The well-known example is that of a nursing home in Illinois, steered on throughput (the number of bedridden patients). The nursing home thus had a strong incentive to keep patients in bed rather than an incentive for quality of care (including getting patients to walk again as soon as possible).[11] Evidently, throughput steering also gives rise to its own strategic behaviour: intensification of the number of internal actions which do not improve eventual performance.

Performance steering rewards products and is thus an incentive for performance: neither the good intention nor the diligent effort, but the result is rewarded. Research conducted at my own university shows, for example, that the introduction of an output model for the allocation of budgets has led to a rise in the number of scientific publications: a rise by 50 per cent in total over a three-year period, in spite of a 5 per cent fall in scientific staff.[12] Other public organizations, too, report a link between the introduction of performance measurement and an increase in production, for example in municipalities[13] and in higher education.[14] When professionals are innovative and enterprising ('I-professionals'), there may be no need for such an incentive. However, there are also routine professionals ('R-professionals')[15]; professional autonomy may degenerate into a non-committal attitude. Performance measurement can make this visible and be an incentive for performance. It is worth noting, however, that being output-oriented will give a professional organization a great deal of autonomy. This is because the question how a product is made (throughput) is less relevant to the director.

This cluster of arguments carries the risk that every reasoning to the contrary carries: input and throughput steering are a disincentive for performance, *and this is why* output steering should be chosen. I will set out in Chapter 2 that output steering can also be a disincentive for performance.

5 Performance measurement improves the quality of policy and decision making

A third cluster of arguments concerns the relation between policy and implementation. Performance measurement in implementing organizations may substantially improve the quality of policy and decision making.

The occasionally awkward relation between policy and implementation partly results from the – necessarily – autonomous position of professional units. This autonomy can then – consciously or unconsciously – be used to justify limited accountability or no accountability at all. This leads to strictly separated worlds of policy making and implementation respectively.

Performance measurement is a strong incentive for external accountability: an implementing organization must make its own goals and performance clear. Consequently, the policy making part of an organization will, in time, have a great deal of quantitative information available about performance. The American Department of Health and Human Services has 300 programmes with a total of 750 'performance goals', made measurable by a multiple of that in performance indicators. This brings many disadvantages, of course, –

see Chapter 2 – but the advantage is that this abundance of goals generates a lot of information about implementation. This information may help the experienced policy maker to appraise performance or to design policy, particularly when he can act with a certain reserve. The reason is that the information will always contain a number of contradictions and will always be one-sided and unreliable as well. So the information will not lead to concrete statements, but it does contribute to the aim of making policy as 'evidence-based' as possible.[16]

Performance measurement thus improves the necessary intertwining of policy making and implementation and also improves the quality of policy and decision making by managerial echelons.

This external orientation is also important because many public organizations depend on each other for their own production. In the chain of criminal procedure, for example, the public prosecution service's production heavily depends on police production. A police organization that is able to provide clarity about its output (both long-term trends and short-term 'real time' information) will allow the public prosecution service to predict its input better and thus arrange its production process better. Something similar applies to the relation between the public prosecution service and the courts: the output of the one is the input of the other.

6 Objections to performance measurement

It is not so difficult to raise a number of objections to the idea that an authority generates measurable products. This section will discuss a number of frequently raised objections, represented in Table 1.1.[17] I will then demonstrate how these objections are dealt with in the thinking about performance measurement. I would like to point out, however, that this enumeration is not meant to show that performance measurement is impossible, but to problematize the overly simple use of performance measurement.

Obligations and values, no products

An authority does not provide products, but fulfils a number of obligations. For example, it safeguards the liveability and safety of a society. In many cases it is responsible for difficult, insoluble problems; dealing with them by an authority is inherently ineffective and inefficient. Constitutional values impose limits on the production of an authority (the effectiveness and efficiency of the prosecution service is restricted by a suspect's legal protection).

Table 1.1 Conditions under which performance measurement is possible and problematic

Performance measurement possible	Performance measurement problematic
An organization has products	An organization has obligations and is highly value-oriented
Products are simple	Products are multiple
An organization is product-oriented	An organization is process-oriented
Autonomous production	Co-production: products are generated together with others
Products are isolated	Products are interwoven
Causalities are known	Causalities are unknown
Quality definable in performance indicators	Quality not definable in performance indicators
Uniform products	Variety of products
Environment is stable	Environment is dynamic

All this is inconsistent with the logic of performance measurement. Performance measurement invites continuous improvement in effectiveness and efficiency. For some public tasks, this is equivalent to a reinforcement of legitimacy. There is no objection to performance measurement then. As regards other public tasks, a conflict exists between effectiveness and efficiency on the one hand and legitimacy on the other hand. Performance measurement of such tasks will encounter problems.

Multiple products, no single products

Products are multiple when they have to do justice to a number of different values, which may also conflict. I have already mentioned the examples of the school and the court earlier, in Section 1. Performance measurement carries the risk of an authority ignoring some of these values (it only meets clearly definable and quantifiable performance goals) and thus not presenting a proper picture of its performance.

Process-oriented, not product-oriented

Certain public organizations are highly process-oriented. Organizations making policies in an environment comprising many parties should invest heavily in consultations and negotiations with these parties. The outcome of such negotiations may be difficult to predict; a good process may yield disappointing products. Something similar applies to research institutes: the products of innovative research are difficult to predict. A well-devised and well-performed research process may nevertheless yield either limited products or no products at all. When processes dominate, performance measurement is pointless.

Products are produced together with others; the authority is not an autonomous producer

The performance of many public organizations are relational: it is achieved in co-production with third parties. The length of a criminal case before a court partly depends on the stance taken by defence counsel; a school's performance partly depends on the attitude of the parents.

Consequently, performance resulting from co-production can only partly be ascribed to public organizations. Performance measurement is based on the idea of an authority being an autonomous producer. Many a system of performance measurement wrongly links the performance achieved and measured to the organization's effort, which produces an incorrect picture.

Products are interwoven, not isolated

Products of public organizations may interfere. The performance of a municipality's spatial planning department may affect the municipality's environmental performance. When a spatial planning directorate is measured chiefly on its own products, it has no incentive to invest in good coordination with the environment directorate. An individual organization scoring high on its own indicators may therefore harm the whole; performance measurement may thus reinforce existing compartmentalization within an organization.

Causalities are unknown or 'contested', not objective

The relation between effort and result is not always known. The interview with a prisoner, aimed at preventing recidivism, is just one of the factors determining whether or not he will reoffend. Where such causalities are unknown or contested, there may be either of two consequences. The product (in the example: no recidivism) is only partly the result of the effort made, which means that the measurement does not produce an adequate picture of the performance of the organization concerned. The organization may respond by choosing to formulate other products (for example: the number of interviews conducted), but these, too, provide no adequate picture of the organization's performance.

***Quality measurement requires a rich picture, performance
measurement leads to a poor picture***

The quality of a great deal of public performance is difficult to
establish with the help of performance indicators. If performance
measurement is nevertheless used, there is a risk that attention to
quantity kills attention to quality. It is worth noting, however, that in
certain performance systems it is undesirable for quality to be
measured. Dutch performance measurement of courts deliberately
does not measure quality because this would affect the judiciary's
independence.

Even the same type of performance shows variety, not uniformity

The same performance may have different meaning in different
contexts. A faculty's performance includes its international, scientific
publications. In a diffuse field like systems engineering and policy
analysis, with a fragmented scientific community, acceptance of a
publication means something different from acceptance in a clearly
delineated field like theoretical physics, with a close-knit scientific
community and an unambiguous language. If the same product can
have a totally different meaning in different contexts, performance
measurement will present an incorrect picture of reality. Performance
measurement will then invite comparison of types of performance
that are incomparable in principle.

The environment is dynamic, not static

Some of the above objections become even more serious when an
organization's environment is dynamic. When the behaviour of the
co-products of an authority keeps changing, when other forms of
intertwining must be established continually or causalities keep
changing due to the behaviour of third parties, the possibilities for
good performance measurement will decrease. The possibilities to
compare performance over a certain time will also decrease.
Performance measurement is based on the tacit assumption that the
environment of public organizations is stable.

7 How do performance measurement systems meet these objections?

The above characteristics of public products do not a priori lead to
the conclusion that performance measurement by authorities is impossible or undesirable. The literature about performance measurement

recognizes these characteristics and also indicates directions in which performance measurement systems should develop, enabling them to cope with the special nature of public products.

7.1 Fine-tuning and limitation of a system's reach

The first direction will be sought within the performance measurement system: 'fine-tuning' of performance measurement and limiting the reach of the system. 'Fine-tuning' can be achieved in various ways.

- Of course, a number of products should always be distinguished for each public organization. Anyone who thinks for a second about the products of a certain public organization will nearly always arrive at a fairly large set of indicators. The product of a court, for example, is the settlement of a case. The Dutch system of performance measurement distinguishes forty-eight types of case settlement.[18] These forty-eight products are generated by distinguishing types of cases and types of settlements.
- There is not one best indicator for each product; an organization should always use a variety of indicators.[19] There are short-term indicators and long-term ones, for productivity, for effectiveness and for efficiency. It is important that there should always be a mix of such indicators, which can furthermore be defined from various perspectives (clients, politicians, professionals, etc.).[20] The reason is that an organization can only confine itself to one or just a few indicators at the expense of the indicators not included in a performance measurement system.[21]
- In addition to product indicators there are process indicators. Performance by particular (parts of) public organizations are 'enabling factors' for the eventual product of public organizations.[22] For such activities, process indicators are more interesting than product indicators.
- 'Fine-tuning' also means that performance measurement takes account of the period needed to generate a product. More often than not, performance measurement is linked to a one-year budget cycle, although achieving the performance takes a longer time.[23] Performance measurement should match the natural cycle for the generation of a product. It is worth noting that this is an argument in favour of decoupling performance measurement and the budget cycle to some extent.

Fine-tuning is almost automatically accompanied by the recognition that performance measurement has a limited reach. There are public products that do not lend themselves to inclusion in a system of performance measurement. Consequently, almost every system identifies a number of products that are placed outside the system. In the above-mentioned system for the judiciary, megacases have explicitly been excluded from the system. Although the settlement of such a case is a product, they are so exceptional that there is no point in including them in a system. Another risk of fine-tuning is, of course, that the system will become too large (this is occasionally referred to 'mushrooming': the attempt to do justice to all imaginable varieties in an organization leads to an explosion of indicators).[24] Consequently, there are limits to doing justice to the variety of an organization, which also leads to the conclusion that the reach of performance measurement is always limited. Measured performance is always an approximation of reality.

7.2 Output in addition to outcome; quality in addition to quantity

Second, it is emphasized that the result of performance measurement will not produce useful knowledge until it is placed in a context. This context can be created by paying attention not only to output, but also to outcome, and by undertaking qualitative analyses in addition to quantitative analyses.

Output measurements involve measurable products of an organization, for example the number of interviews a probation officer conducts with prisoners.

Output does not acquire meaning until it is related to outcome: the eventual, envisaged, but more remote effect (for recidivism: whether or not the ex-prisoner reoffends as a result of the interviews). The measurement of the outcome frequently requires further research (for example: a 'public focus group' in a client survey). Supplementing output figures with details about the outcome produces a richer picture of the performance. However, a richer picture may be a less unambiguous picture; specifying the relation between output and outcome will be difficult in many cases.

A system of performance measurement cannot do without qualitative analyses. Naturally, this is true in the first place of performance that cannot be quantified. Qualitative analyses are also important for performance that can be expressed in indicators. This is because a meaning has to be attached to this performance, and this meaning does not automatically result from the production targets.

This is recognized in nearly all the literature about performance measurement. Many writers postulate that performance measurements can be an important 'trigger' to obtain this type of qualitative information. Performance measurement produces no 'dials' (scales from which performance may be read), but only 'tin-openers', which invite further research.[25] The idea is that anyone with performance measurements at their disposal can use them to form an initial picture about performance and can also examine for what performance more qualitative information is desirable. Performance measurement provides no answers, but inspires us to ask the right questions.[26] This reasoning is a sympathetic one, but also carries some major risks, to which I shall refer later in Chapter 6. Furthermore, although performance measurement may in theory be given a limited place as a 'tin-opener', in practice there is a strong temptation to use it as 'dial' all the same. I shall refer to this, too, in Chapter 3.

7.3 Performance measurement facilitates decision making, but does not direct it

In the third place, performance measurement does not steer appraisal of the performance of an organization, but facilitates it. It is one of the sources of information that can play a role in the appraisal of the performance of an organization and may thus produce a rich picture about this performance.

An organization can learn about its own performance by being confronted with information about output, outcome and qualitative information. Certain conclusions must be drawn when these three sources present the same picture. Entirely different conclusions drawn from these sources would force an organization to reflect and find out the reason. This, too, is a form of learning.

Performance measurement plays a more facilitating role here, but is indispensable in forming a picture about the performance. The reason is that appraisal exclusively based on statements about quality and outcome is, by definition, highly coloured by the perspective of the person who formulates these statements (since causalities and quality are not open to objectification). If this is the case, strategic behaviour often lurks beneath the surface: statements are made about outcome and quality that suit the speaker's interest. In both cases, quantified information about products can act as a 'countervailing power', it could be used for critical reflection when an appraisal is based merely on quantity and outcome.

Suppose, for example, that a police organization invests a lot of manpower in a neighbourhood housing many ethnic young people and in which there were law and order problems for many years. After one year, the public order problems are a thing of the past (outcome), but the police officers involved score low in the output model that is used: few people have been reported, few arrests have been made, few information campaigns, etc. This discrepancy is interesting and can prompt at least two questions: is the contribution by the police officers involved still required (the ethnic community may have taken its own measures) or do the police officers achieve a performance whose output is difficult to measure (for example, do they invest a lot of effort in maintaining relations with the residents in the neighbourhood). When these questions are asked, a picture will form that is more interesting than in a situation where mere output is examined (conclusion: non-performance) or mere outcome is examined (conclusion: top performance).

This use of performance measurements will only come about when an organization organizes them very well, for example by scrutinizing the confrontation between various sources of information systematically in an audit process. In the design of such a process, the order will often be that an organization is invited to give an appraisal itself about its own performance based on the three sources of information (output, outcome and quantitative information), after which top management itself forms an appraisal. Both appraisals are then compared and the management can make a statement about performance. The more complex the products of an organization (see the dimensions listed in Section 6), the more limited the role performance management is likely to play.

2 The perverse effects of performance measurement

1 Introduction

The positive effects of performance measurement were discussed in Chapter 1. Performance measurement is an incentive for production, for innovation, for adequate accountability and it reinforces an organization's external orientation. There is another picture, however, apart from this beneficial effect of performance measurement: performance measurement creates a large number of perverse effects. I shall outline these effects in this chapter (Sections 2–6) and I shall give an initial explanation for them (Sections 7–10). I shall then indicate in Chapter 3 that the perverse effects will nearly always come to dominate the beneficial effects in the long term. This eventually prompts the question how performance measurement can be designed so as to neutralize the perverting effects as much as possible.

2 Performance measurement is a stimulus to strategic behaviour

Performance measurement may be an important stimulus to a public organization's productivity. This is because the organization's production will at least be made visible, and it may also be sanctioned for it (depending on the functions assigned to performance measurement).

There is another picture, however: measuring and rewarding products may be an important incentive for strategic behaviour. A public organization increases its production in accordance with the system's criteria, but this increase in production has no significance or has a negative significance from a professional perspective. This form of strategic behaviour is sometimes referred to as 'gaming the numbers'.[1] Here are a number of examples:

- The production figures of Groningen's Public Prosecution Service show that it drops considerably fewer cases than in the preceding years. A reduction in the number of cases dropped is one of the Minister of Justice's goals; the service that succeeds in reducing the number of cases dropped will receive a bonus. So this is a successful form of performance measurement. Actually a Public Prosecution Service employee already deletes a large number of offences from the computer at the police station, thus reducing the number of cases that reach the Public Prosecution Service, which partly accounts for the positive figure mentioned above. The numbers are thus reduced artificially, qualifying the Public Prosecution Service for the financial bonus awarded by the Department. The Prosecution Service employees referred to are called 'filterers' in Groningen; the phenomenon also occurs in Amsterdam, where they are referred to as 'hoppers'.[2]

- One performance indicator for the American FBI is the number of arrests. A constant increase in the performance required invites strategic behaviour. The FBI proves capable of reaching higher and higher production figures as regards arrests by arresting deserters from the armed forces. They are easier to detect than other lawbreakers. These arrests hardly serve any social purpose and are only made to meet the performance standards. As a result, the percentage of detainees that is actually prosecuted is extremely low, because performance is trivial.[3]

- A particular department in the Australian army is responsible for housing servicemen stationed far from home. After a first interview, the unit makes the serviceman in question an offer as soon as possible. When he declines the offer, the unit registers his reasons and makes a second offer. This procedure is repeated when he declines again. The performance indicator for this unit is defined at some stage as the percentage of servicemen accepting a house after a maximum of three offers. This percentage turns out to be 100 per cent in less than no time. The explanation is simple: the unit introduces the phenomenon of an 'informal offer' and does not make a formal offer until it is sure that it will be accepted.[4]

There is strategic behaviour here because the above-mentioned performance only exists on paper. The performance has no social significance or just a very limited one. From the perspective of the organization in question, however, the above course of action may be absolutely legitimate. Acquiring a budget allocation as efficiently as possible is a legitimate activity. The behaviour of the 'filterers' can also be defined as a way of clearing statistics and adding meaning to them or even as a form of chain care. What is strategic behaviour from a social point of view may be prudent behaviour on the level of the individual organization. This is an important fact, because it hampers a moral appeal to the organization concerned to refrain from such behaviour.

3 Performance measurement blocks innovations and ambitions

An organization faced with performance measurement will make an effort to optimize its production process, allowing it to achieve its performance as efficiently as possible, particularly when performance measurement is linked to some form of financial reward. This may be a strong incentive to think in 'cash cows': what products are relatively easy to make, enabling as much money as possible to be generated?

Thinking in cash cows means that an organization minimizes its throughput, nearly always at the expense of *innovation*. Anyone wishing to innovate will explore the unknown and accepts the risk that the results may be either what was expected or less than expected. Innovation may therefore harm an organization's production. Performance measurement rewards the constant reproduction of the existing.[5]

One example of this is a research group on public finance within a university. The researchers have specialized in research into levies for a number of years. They have acquired considerable expertise in the subject and are able to publish articles about the subject relatively quickly and simply, both in national and international journals. The system of performance measurement rewards them richly for it. Innovation – searching for new research themes – will cause a drop in the number of publications (and therefore in income) after some years because new research will take a number of years to start a steady flow of publications.[6]

The phenomenon that organizations raise their performance by optimizing their input is well-known, too. The selection standard for input is that it demands the lowest possible throughput to obtain the desired output. Empirical research also reveals this form of behaviour, known as 'creaming' or 'cherry picking'.

- Schools that are rewarded for performance (laid down in a 'charter' between the funding authority and the school's management) or functioning in a 'voucher system' (spending the vouchers partly depends on the school's performance) have been found to select their input. They manage to keep out potential pupils with learning or behavioural problems or successfully use a 'counselling out' strategy.[7] The school's performance thus goes up, causing the agreements in the charter to be easier to meet or raising the chances that parents will opt for this school. As a

result, the variety of the pupil population within schools will fall
below an educationally desirable level.[8]

• An example too nice to omit: the fight against muskrats can be
  based on a bonus system. People receive a certain amount of
  money for every dead muskrat they catch and hand in. This
  performance is included in many municipal performance surveys.
  Here, too, the phenomenon of input optimization occurs: 'Why
  should you catch two rats in winter, if there might be thirty of
  them in spring, parents and offspring together?'[9]

An organization optimizing its input does so at the expense of its
ambitions. An organization needs to put in less effort to achieve a
desirable output if it manipulates the quality or quantity of the input.

4 Performance measurement veils actual performance

Performance measurement also serves to allow an organization to
account for its performance and is an important tool to slightly
objectify its (public) account. It enables a controlling body (a Board
of Management, a regulator, a chosen body) to penetrate into the
capillaries of an organization.

Performance measurement may also veil an organization's performance, however. The higher the extent to which information is
aggregated, the remoter it is from the primary process, where it was
generated. Consequently, insight may be lost into the causal connections that exist on the level of the primary process (and give a
meaning to the figures). The director only sees the aggregated data
and runs the risk of construing his own causalities from them.[10] In
other words, performance measurement casts a veil.

It may be added that the production figure that produces a picture
on the level of the whole (macro), is always an average and therefore
cannot simply be applied to the individual parts (micro) that have
provided information for this aggregated picture. If causalities are
nevertheless construed on the basis of the aggregated data, or if
macro-pictures are directly translated to the micro-level, the risk is
that injustice will be done to performance.

• A scientist publishes an article about the swimming behaviour of
  dolphins in an international biological journal. On average,
  articles in this journal are cited forty times in four years. The
  article in question is cited only six times. This results in a low
  score for the article. The error here is that a macro-picture (the
  average score of articles in the journal) is applied to the micro-

level (the concrete article about dolphins). It is then found that only six articles about the swimming behaviour of dolphins appeared in the four years concerned (in all of which the above article was indeed cited).[11] All this will only be different if the aim of the measurement is to find out whether research into the swimming behaviour of dolphins is a research subject that belongs to the core of the scientist's activities.

This mechanism goes hand in hand with another mechanism: the bigger the distance between the person producing production figures and the person using production figures, the more reliable the figures are taken to be. The professional producing a production figure is close to the primary process and knows the reality behind the figure. The production figure is one of the sources of information which acquires a meaning in combination with other (in many cases qualitative) sources of information. The production figure is far more important as a source of information for a director who is far removed from this primary process, and quantitative details by definition invite being regarded as reliable and incontestable. If these figures are indeed regarded as reliable figures, the director in question will feel justified in carrying out interventions based on them. Anyone who asks for the reality behind the figures or for the assumptions and aggregation rules used will soon call the suspicion on himself that he does not want to face the facts.

- Research by Bowerman and Hawksworth into performance measurement among local authorities demonstrates this mechanism. They conclude that external reviewers collect the information about the performance of local authorities and that it is often dealt with in a rigid way. Directives based on comparisons between authorities are issued about performance or about savings that may be achieved in individual municipalities. This rigid attitude denies that 'what is true in general may not be true universally and without qualification because circumstances alter cases'. Once it is clear that performance measurement is used in this way, the result is predictable: performance measurement is a form of nuisance to local authorities; they should try to prevent it as much as possible.[12]

A measured performance can thus have two meanings: the meaning given on the level of the primary process and the meaning given to the performance at managerial level. This fact, in turn, invites various forms of strategic behaviour.

5 Performance measurement kills the professional attitude: no quality, no system responsibility, more bureaucracy

Public products and services are always a trade-off between a number of values, as they are in the private sector.[13] A museum that builds up a collection works from a variety of interests: its collection should have cultural value, should preserve heritage, serves an educational purpose, should make (future) scientific research possible and should serve the public. The essence of the museum profession is the constant trade-off made between these interests, which may conflict.

Performance indicators measure quantities and will therefore mainly be applied to measurable and clearly definable interests; for museums these are the numbers of visitors. As regards the other interests (scientific research, for example), the performance indicators are always a derivative (the number of documents consulted by researchers, for example). The result is predictable: when only visitor numbers are relevant, the integrity of the collection will suffer.[14] Performance measurement not only leads to a distorted image of professional performance (Section 4), but it may also kill the professional attitude because the museum concentrates too much on the well-defined tasks.[15]

- I refer here to a remarkable study by Iaquinto, which is illustrative even though it concerns the private sector. Iaquinto examined the influence of winning the Deming prize for 'total quality management' (TQM) by Japanese companies on their performance. He found that at the vast majority of them the winning of the award is followed by a drop in performance. For TQM, a large number of performance indicators exist, which are always a derivative, since it concerns the 'contested' concept of quality. Companies take three years to maximize their performance on these indicators. Consequently, they will focus strongly on these indicators for a longer time and neglect other aspects of their business operations. The result is that their performance will decline. Focusing on performance indicators kills the professional attitude of seeking constant trade-offs between different interests.[16]
- The system operating within the judiciary identifies products and allocates a normative time compensation to each product. An application for attachment is dealt with by the president of the court. An application for a garnishee order, for example, will have to filed by a procurator *litis* (a lawyer registered at the court in question). It must appear summarily from the application that

there is a claim and that it is feared that the debtor will cause property for which recourse is available to be lost. The debtor is not heard; he will not become aware of the application until the attachment is actually levied. An application to the president has a low weighting factor: 15 minutes for the judge and 15 minutes for the staff.

There are courts that spend a lot of time and effort dealing with applications of this kind; not only do they examine the application itself, but they are likely to seek further information from the applicant as well. This causes some applications to be turned down, but it also has a certain steering effect: in this court unwarranted applications (in fact unlawful debt collection activities) evidently stand a lower chance of success.

There are also courts that hardly examine an application at all and in fact grant applications for attachment as a standard procedure. An application to lift the attachment may then be filed, which will be dealt with as interlocutory proceedings. If an application for attachment has in fact been used as disguised debt collection and the claim and/or the fear that property for which recourse is available may be caused to be lost are rightfully disputed, the president will lift the attachment. This does not take a lot of court time and writing a judgment (if it is not passed orally) will not take much time either. Such a judgment in interlocutory proceedings has a weighting factor of 190 minutes for the judge and 675 minutes for the staff.

An attachment order seriously affects the party against which the attachment order is made, particularly if it is a business. For example, it can no longer use its bank account. The judgment debtor must bring in a lawyer, who must issue a writ of summons in interlocutory proceedings. This takes time, but it is also an expensive exercise. Even if the case is won, only part of the costs will be refunded. A debt collection attachment is rarely successful. When cases are clear and major interests are at stake, the interlocutory proceedings route is likely to be chosen.

A court that, from a professional perspective, follows the correct procedure (taking a critical look at an attachment application) will, in this system, be worse off in the final analysis. A great deal of time is spent on an action with a low weighting factor. The system in fact rewards courts that do not filter cases: the application is dealt with in the time available and the interlocutory proceedings to lift an attachment also earn the court a profit.[17]

This forcing-out mechanism may also occur among organizations. Particularly in the public sector, organizations have a *system responsibility*. Organizations should make the professional insights they develop available to other organizations in the public sector. Performance measurement may force out this system responsibility.

- Research by Fiske and Ladd showed that schools competing with each other in terms of performance are less prepared to share their 'best practices' (regarding methods of education, how to deal with differences between pupils, health, etc.) with each other. Performance measurement has a negative influence on the relations that schools maintain with each other.[18]

The underlying mechanism here is that performance measurement forces an organization to optimize its own performance. This makes performance measurement a disincentive for cooperation. It may consequently lead to *compartmentalization* (compartments optimize their own performance and cooperate insufficiently) or block various forms of *chain cooperation*.

- Research also shows that organizations scoring well in a system of performance measurement have invested heavily in procedural and organizational amenities, thus enabling them to meet the requirements of the system of performance measurement.[19] There is a separate department, for example, that registers each product of an organization and sees to it that the individual members of the organization provide it with all the information.

Now there is no objection to this at all, although the research mentioned also shows that, on paper, these organizations do perform better than organizations having fewer such amenities, but do not do so in reality.

The explanation is easy to guess: a department whose main task is to register and account for an organization's performance is likely to be competent to do it so as to allow its own organization to score as well as possible in the system.

- Research by Power points in that direction. Organizations in the United Kingdom prove to be adept at massaging reality in such a way that it becomes accessible to the controller. Making information 'auditable' has a higher priority than actually solving problems.[20] One beneficial effect of performance measurement is that it may reinforce an organization's external orientation (see

Chapter 1). It may now be stated that the picture may also be the reverse: performance measurement may also reinforce an organization's internal orientation.

6 Performance measurement leads to punishment of performance

Performance measurement rewards productivity, but its effect may also be that productivity is punished. There are four mechanisms that account for this effect.

Everybody performs better and therefore receives a financial sanction

First, if performance measurement is linked to a financial reward, there is an incentive for the organizations concerned to increase productivity. This increase in productivity does not lead to reward, however, if the budget to be divided among these organizations remains the same. This is a well-known problem: there is a previously fixed price per product, and the organizations concerned increase their total production to such a level that the budgets allocated to the organizations exceed the total budget available. The result may be that management must cut prices per product later, after production has been established. This may create the impression that better performance is not rewarded.

A transparent and well-performing organization is vulnerable

Performance measurement leads to transparency and may be an incentive for production. This may cause a rise in production on a given budget and, the reasoning will go, the same performance can probably be achieved on a lower budget. Bordewijk and Klaassen point to the phenomenon that an organization that invests in efficiency is taking a risk: management may translate this into a lower budget for the next year, performance remaining equal. An affiliate organization not investing in efficiency is rewarded with a budget that remains the same, performance remaining equal.[21]

The mechanism here is that thanks to transparency and good performance, higher targets may be imposed, whereas an organization that is unable to offer this transparency (in the worst case because it performs badly) is 'rewarded' with equal targets and resources. In time, this creates the impression that good performance is punished and poor performance is rewarded. If this impression becomes embedded, it warrants various other forms of perverting behaviour.

An organization performs better in a non-performing environment and therefore receives a financial sanction (1)

When the various organizations show approximately the same rise in productivity, it would be unfair for budgets to remain the same: a cut in the price per product. Everybody suffers this injustice to the same degree, however.

A different situation arises when particular organizations show a rise in productivity while other organizations seriously lag behind them. This causes the well-performing organizations to grow and the non-performing ones to fall behind (entirely in line with the aims of performance measurement). At some stage, the non-performing part of the organization approaches a critical lower limit. The ultimate consequence of performance measurement would be that the 'non-performer' disappears, but in many situations that is impossible.

This is because such a consequence presupposes that the superior has a sufficient degree of freedom to take such a measure. Frequently, this is not the case: a drastic intervention is subject to all sorts of (legal) constraints. This has an important consequence: the cost of punishing non-performance is likely to be higher than the benefit of rewarding performance.

It may be added that the cause and effect of non-performance may be debatable. What is the explanation for the situation in which the non-performing part of the organization has ended up? Two opposite lines of reasoning are imaginable:

- The organization fails to perform. The system of performance measurement makes this visible and draws its conclusions. The cause of the situation in which the organization finds itself is therefore the poor performance of this organization part.
- The organization fails to perform. The cause of it is the system of performance measurement. When performance is below standard, the system applies a financial sanction. This means that the resources of the relevant organization part will diminish, causing performance to fall even further, causing another financial sanction, and so on. Performance measurement means that the rich are getting richer and the poor are getting poorer.

The management of an organization thus has to make a trade-off, the outcome of which is predictable:

- The cost of punishing non-performance is higher than that of rewarding good performance.

- There is a line of reasoning available that concludes that the system of performance measurement is the cause of the poor performance.

The result of this reasoning is that the non-performing organization part is offered help, in some cases at the expense of the well-performing organization part. The reasoning may be correct, but it may also be an occasional argument. If the latter is the case, there is a performance paradox: any party performing well in a non-performing environment will eventually get punished.

An organization performs better in a non-performing environment and therefore receives a financial sanction (2)

A variant of this mechanism occurs in organizations providing substitutable products and services. If this is the case, there is a strong incentive for performance in such organizations. After all, in the event of non-performance the director has an alternative: he can substitute the products and services of organization part A for those of organization part B.

An organization part providing non-substitutable products and services has a weaker incentive for performance because it is a monopolist. It is not attractive for the director to punish non-performance of such an organization part, since this will cause problems: the product or the service can no longer be provided. This gives rise to an incentive structure as summarized in Table 2.1.

In a mixed environment – both substitutable and non-substitutable products and services – the incentive structure also suggests that performance is not rewarded. One organization part has strong incentives for performance and is punished if it fails to perform; the other organization part will suffer hardly any consequences of non-performance.

Table 2.1 Performance measurement involving substitutable and non-substitutable products

	Performance measurement from the perspective of the organization part	*Performance measurement from the management's perspective*
Product/ service substitutable	Incentive to perform	Incentive to sanction
Product/ service not substitutable	No incentive to perform	No incentive to sanction

The last two mechanisms make clear that performance measurement does not work when sharp differences exist between organizations. This is a paradoxical conclusion: performance measurement stimulates performance, but only if the levels of performance by the organizations do not differ too much. In many cases, this causes performance measurement to be designed in such a way that it cannot cause excessive differences between organizations. This can be realized by all sorts of moderating mechanisms or by defining performance indicators so as to take expected differences in performance into account beforehand.

7 Explanations

What is the explanation for the above picture? Why do systems of performance measurement create the above, perverse effects? Even when performance measurement is designed in the way described in Chapter 1?

Systems of performance measurement are inconsistent with three developments facing the public sector:

- increasing professional development of the services rendered by the authority;
- increasing intertwining of public organizations and other organizations;
- increasing variety within public organizations.

This conflict causes performance measurement to pervert even in an organization comprising only very honest professionals. What is more, it will pervert in just that organization.

7.1 Professional development: performance measurement is poor

The most important characteristic of a professional organization is that the primary process is complex and knowledge-intensive. This has a number of consequences for the organization shaping this process:[22]

- The primary process requires special *expertise,* which is difficult to standardize. This makes an organization always highly dependent on the expertise of the organization's members. Much of the expertise is 'tacit knowledge': it is difficult to specify and to formalize.
- Earlier I mentioned the need to make trade-offs. Professional activities like those of a museum director are *multiple*: they must

do justice to several values or interests that may conflict. Such a trade-off should always meet the standard of 'locality': it should match the special circumstances of a concrete case and may therefore differ from one situation to another. This is why a fixed standard for the trade-off is not available in most cases.

- A public service professional provides services by *interacting* with the environment (citizens, companies, other authorities, fellow professionals). Organizing this interaction and using it to improve the quality of the services rendered is part of this professionalism.
- A professional is adaptive and will learn. New developments are linked to his existing expertise, which creates new expertise. Expertise develops in processes of interaction between a professional and his environment.[23] This makes professional development an ongoing *process*.
- Finally, professional expertise and skills are difficult to transfer. In many cases, a professional himself will only learn by interacting with third parties (since his expertise is 'tacit' and frequently does not become explicit until he interacts with third parties). Professionalism is also difficult to teach, isolated as it is from the concrete performance of a professional activity. Every form of formalization of the profession (in handbooks, manuals, but also in formal systems of accountability) fails to do sufficient justice to the richness of the profession.

Each of these characteristics is inconsistent with a system of performance measurement. I shall work this out using an example from the police organization.[24]

Three armed raids have occurred in a shopping centre over a four-month period. This has caused unrest and the question is what action the police should take in the area concerned. The answer depends on, for example:

- the geographical composition of the neighbourhood;
- the shopping patterns;
- the extent to which the shopkeepers are organized;
- the urgency of other problems facing the area team;
- the architectural design of the shopping centre.

A police official's first opinion about the most effective strategy will be based on these and many other considerations. It results partly from objectifiable facts and circumstances, partly from the professional's 'tacit knowledge': his experience of this type of crime in this neighbourhood. When various police officials, each with their own 'tacit knowledge', exchange their experiences and knowledge, a rich image of an effective strategy emerges. The choice of the eventual strategy is made by interacting with the actors directly involved (the management of the shopping centre's car park, the shopkeepers' association, the shopping centre's security firm, municipal departments). The outcome of these consultations is a number of agreements with these actors meant bring about a drop in the number of raids.

This strategy development is a learning process: the strategy is adjusted on the basis of the experiences of other professionals and the views of the actors concerned. This process of interaction continues when the agreements are implemented: the professionals and actors concerned form an image of the effects of the agreements and adjust them where necessary.

The idea underlying performance measurement is that performance of public organizations may be standardized in a set of performance indicators. This is inconsistent with the professional character of many public organizations. From the professional's perspective, the application of performance measurement to professional processes leads to *poor information*.

- The police organization's strategy comprises a large number of actions. This rich image is only partly reflected in the performance measurement, however. This may lead to the judgment that no justice is done to the professional's expertise. A system of performance measurement will never produce a rich image of professional activities.
- An adequate appraisal of the strategy of the police organization should also reckon with the 'throughput': the efforts made by the organization to arrive at an effective strategy with the parties concerned. In output thinking this is just expenditure to arrive at the product; in professional thinking they are crucial to the appraisal of the police's approach.
- When services are rendered by interacting with the actors concerned, the eventual performance also depends on the effort of the other actors. As a rule, systems of performance measurement do not recognize this.

The fact that a system of performance measurement is experienced as poor justifies the instrumental use of it. The idea then is that performance measurement is not suitable to arrive at a meaningful appraisal of performance. It is nevertheless used by management, which justifies the professional in utilizing the possibilities offered by the

Table 2.2 The relation between performance and accounting for it

	Good	Bad
Performance	I	II
Accounting for it	III	IV

system in an opportunistic way. Once such a course of action has developed, it may become institutionalized in course of time: opportunistic use is perfectly normal and is therefore no longer regarded as opportunism.

The poor character of the information that performance measurement produces has a paradoxical effect, represented in Table 2.2.

Performance measurement may result in the following two combinations, however strange at first sight.

- *Performance good, accounting for it bad.* A professional achieving a good performance is then asked to account for it in a poor system. For a well-performing professional, this makes a system of performance measurement an important disincentive to account for his actions.
- *Performance poor, accounting for it good.* The poorly performing professional may manage to make his performance look fairly respectable in a poor system. This mechanism is mentioned in the literature: 'Our worst centers are those that are number-driven – if the goal is 250 (. . .), you can be sure that they will enroll 252'.[25] Performance measurement sometimes offers the possibility to do so.

7.2 Intertwining: performance measurement is unfair

The use of performance measurement may be based on the assumption that a public organization can be run as a project:

- identify problems;
- formulate goals to solve these problems;
- define performance indicators for the implementing organizations;
- implement the goals;
- measure whether the agreed performance has been achieved;
- evaluate and appraise.

This way of thinking tends to have a hierarchical undertone: management formulates problems, goals and indicators, the professionals implement, management measures, evaluates and appraises.

Performance measurement does not recognize the fact that performance is achieved in a network of dependencies. Organizations that must achieve a performance are not autonomous in doing so. It is a matter of co-production with third parties. This is why it is unfair to measure an organization in terms of performance.

A system experienced as 'unfair' invites perverting behaviour. On the one hand, the system does not recognize an organization's dependencies and on the other hand it is used to appraise this organization. As soon as the system offers possibilities to influence the appraisal of an organization part in a positive sense, the chances are that professionals will make use of it.

Performance measurement has a number of functions, which have a rising degree of compulsion: transparency – learn – appraise – sanction. The more performance measurement is used compulsively, the more it will be experienced as unfair and the more it will cause perverting behaviour (see Figure 2.1).

This again creates a paradoxical picture: the more a management wants to steer with the help of performance measurement, the stronger the incentive for the members of the organization to show perverse behaviour. I shall revert to this in Chapter 5 and shall set out what this conclusion means for the design of a system of performance measurement.

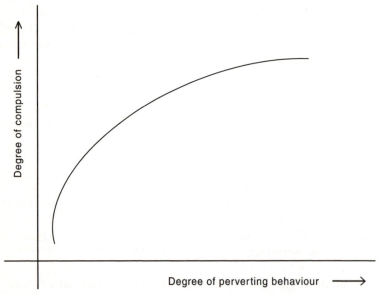

Figure 2.1 Consequences of increasing compulsion in the use of performance measurement for the effectiveness of performance measurement.

7.3 Dynamic: performance measurement is not lively

A third justification for opportunistic use is that a system of performance measurement tends to be static. It considers at a particular moment in time the products supplied at that moment. This does insufficient justice to the dynamic of professional activities.

- New performance does not always match the existing system of performance measurement. New *products* may develop, not visible in the performance measurement, with existing production falling sharply. This might suggest that the performance of the professional in question is declining. But the conclusion is that performance measurement is not lively.
- It is equally important that a great deal of dynamic does not involve the products of the organization, but the *generation processes* that precede it. A university produces a certain output: master's degrees, for example. This production is the result of a process, in which all sorts of things happen due to developments in the university's environment (for example, a new type of student enters, different from earlier types; there are new technological developments). The professional is active in this process and deals with questions that are only partly reflected in production targets. What subjects does the university offer? How intense is the guidance given to students? What additional activities are organized for and with the students? Has the university got an international exchange programme? Does the education involve the use of information and communication technology? How does the university deal with changes in the learning styles of new generations of students? These questions concern the essence of the profession and cause considerable dynamic in professional organizations. Performance measurement systems that fail to address such questions are not lively for a professional.

The more complex a product (for example, it is generated in a network of dependencies; it is multiple, see Table 1.1), the greater the dynamic because more actors are involved and because more values must be weighed. The problem here is that many systems of performance measurement are necessarily static because of the functions for which they are used. When budgets are allocated or a 'benchmark' is made with the help of performance measurement, the system requires a certain stability. Only then is comparison over a certain time possible and can the system fulfil its function. Moreover, the simple solution for dynamic – identify new products and retain the existing products – may be inconsistent with the functions of

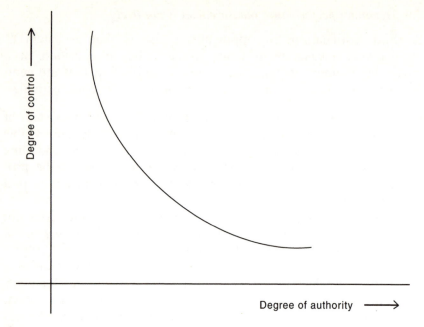

Figure 2.2 Conflict between stability and liveliness/authority of systems of
performance measurement.

performance measurement. This solution easily leads to what was
called 'mushrooming' in Chapter 1: explosive growth in the number of
products and performance indicators, causing the system of
performance measurement to lose its function.

From a professional perspective, dynamic of performance measurement is therefore desirable, from a management and control perspective the accent is on stability. This conflict is represented in
Figure 2.2.

The figure shows the result: the more performance measurement is
used as a management tool, the less authoritative it is for the
professional.

8 Question: how to value the ambiguous image of performance measurement?

The criticism of performance measurement in this chapter is that for
the enterprising professional it is poor, unfair and not lively. This
justifies perverting behaviour: the system is fed with information that
only serves to show up the position of the professional to the best

advantage (strategic behaviour, using the veiling effect of figures, procedural and organizational amenities, optimization of input, minimization of throughput, accepting no system responsibility, sacrificing quality).

The system consequently loses its effectiveness. However, when a system of performance measurement is effective – it influences the professional's behaviour – it also creates perverse effects because of its poor, unfair and static character (no innovation, no ambitions, etc.). An ambiguous picture of performance measurement has now been painted: it may be beneficial, but also cause perverse effects. This raises the question as to how these images relate to each other.

I shall give a first answer in Chapter 3: an important risk is that the perverse effect of performance measurement may eventually force out the beneficial effect. In the following chapters I shall discuss the question of how the conflict between beneficial and perverse effects can be turned to good use.

3 The resistance of perverted performance measurement

1 Introduction

The picture of performance measurement painted so far is an ambiguous one. Performance measurement may have a beneficial effect in the public sector, but may also produce perverse effects. Before entering further into the significance of this conclusion regarding the design of performance measurement, another observation is important, comprising two elements:

- Once a system of performance measurement has been designed and introduced, the perverse effects will, in the long term, force out the beneficial effect.[1]
- The perverted systems of performance measurement developed in this way are nevertheless resistant.

In the following sections (2, 3 and 4) I shall give three explanations for this phenomenon. Section 4 contains a short intermezzo about production measurement in American corporate culture.

2 Performance measurement systems tend to freeze

A first explanation is that a system of performance measurement, once introduced, tends to freeze. Product definitions have been chosen, performance measurement plays its role in the iron rhythm of the planning and control cycle or organizational provisions have been made to collect and aggregate the required information each year. Changing this system proves difficult for a number of reasons.

As a rule, designing a system of performance measurement is a huge effort for an organization. From a *professional* perspective, designing a system requires an organization to define products, develop procedures to count, aggregate and report products and develop procedures to arrive at output appraisal. The mere defining of products, particularly when an organization is not familiar with thinking in terms of products, tends to be a complex activity. For example, the development of a product budget for municipalities may have to meet the following requirements:[2]

- The product budget defines all activities of a municipality in terms of products (output) or desirable effects (outcome).
- The product budget combines and concentrates all necessary information about the individual products.
- The product budget provides measurable standards for both financial and non-financial performance indicators.
- The product budget is fully consistent with other policy and management tools.

Although a more moderate stance is possible and exists in many cases, it will be clear that performance measurement demands considerable effort on the part of an organization. Once such an edifice has been erected and has embedded itself in an organization, changing the system is not easy.

The design of a system also has a *political* dimension. No system evolves 'from scratch' but is developed in existing organizations with an existing balance of power. As a result, systems tend to reflect this balance of power, because the system will only work if the most important players in an organization sufficiently identify themselves with it. This means, for example, that the product definitions and prices per product are chosen so as to give these players at least a fair chance of achieving a good performance or obtain a budget that will be sufficient for them.

If the system results from negotiations, it tends to be a rather complex one: the system contains exceptions, inconsistencies or compensatory and transitional provisions. The system thus represents the interests in the organization. Any infringement of the system may warrant a following amendment and affect support for it. As a result, amendment is undesirable; the system freezes.

The introduction of performance measurement also has an important *temporal* dimension. Designing it and acquiring support for it will take some time, while the transition from an existing system to a new system may easily take a few budget years. Osborne and Plastrik postulate that the full introduction of a system of per-formance measurement takes a period of three to four years.[3] When an organization has invested a lot of time and money in a system, changing the system is not easy. If there was a lot of opposition during the development of the system, this mechanism may be even stronger. Decisions taken after much opposition and doubt tend to be difficult to revoke because nobody wants to go through the painful process of decision making again.[4] The organization has gone to substantial investment to design the system; this is why it deserves protection and, consequently, freezes.

Earlier (in Chapter 2) I referred to an important *instrumental* argument that may cause performance measurement to freeze. If a system is to fulfil its functions (transparency, learning, appraising, sanctioning and comparing), it should be stable. This is because comparisons over a certain time or between organizations are hampered when new elements continue to be added to the system. This will cause 'mushrooming': new products continue to be added to the system. The result is that the system will become too large, contradictions and overlapping product definitions develop, the system's accessibility decreases and the possibilities for strategic behaviour increase. The conclusion is that systems should be kept stable.

Finally, once a system has been introduced, a network of stakeholders will form round this system: the director, who can show results to outsiders, certain professionals who spot a lot of opportunities in the form of performance measurement chosen, and staff departments for which performance measurement is a major activity. Admittedly, this applies to any tool, but for performance measurement a complete 'performance management industry' has developed. Civil servants, accountants, scientists, media and consultants have thrown themselves into the subject and are constantly feeding the debate with new questions or requirements on the one hand and new answers on the other. This is visible in a much bigger form in the United States, which has its Government Performance and Results Act (GPRA). Broere discerns a GPRA industry in Washington: the Office of Management and Budget, the US Court of Audit, the media (which constantly publish the scores of public organizations), the staff of congressmen and senators, employees of the big think tanks, consultants, etc.[5] There is no objection to such an industry, as long as it is sufficiently critical of performance measurement. If it is not, it will promote freezing: a number of players in the organization have an interest in maintaining performance measurement; they are supported by an industry, which also has an interest in maintaining a system of performance measurement and continues to produce new promises, 'challenges' and tools.

Systems that freeze produce the perverse effects from Chapter 2. A frozen system on the one hand poses less and less challenge to organization parts, while on the other hand they can learn better and better how to avoid the steering effect of the system. Organization parts learn what strategic behaviour stands the best chances, how they can optimize input and throughput, what the 'cash cows' are or what administrative provisions are the most lucrative for this part of the organization. This creates a system that produces perverse effects and is nevertheless resistant. Seen from the angle of a system's rationality the stability of a system, once introduced, is quite defensible after all.

3 Performance measurement invites command and control

Although warnings against the hierarchical use of performance measurement abound,[6] writers also conclude that it is very tempting and inviting to use it as a tool for hierarchical steering.[7]

Performance measurement would seem to offer a director a tool to manage complex processes. The complexity of these processes implies that throughput steering is difficult for a director, because he will then have to concern himself with the content of these processes, for which he will often lack the 'in-depth' expertise. Performance measurement means that less interference with the process is needed and suggests that the director may nevertheless provide powerful steering.

- This steering seems *effective*: the director fixes targets, measures output and then appraises the subordinate. Certain handbooks about performance management nourish this idea: 'Performance management sends employees unmistakable signals about what results matter, and rewards them when they produce those results'.[8] Political priorities may be translated into new targets, for example; after a certain period it may be considered whether they are being achieved; adjustment during this period is possible, if required.
- This steering seems *efficient*: performance measurement may cause a director and a professional to become much less inter-related. The director is only interested in output, after all, not in how it is achieved, so intense interaction between the top and the professionals is not required. Performance measurement thus generates much lower interaction costs than input or throughput steering.

Hierarchical use is harmful

Such steering seems effective, but it actually produces perverse effects.[9] This is a first paradox of the hierarchical use of performance measurement: the stronger hierarchical steering, the fewer results, because the incentives to cause the system to pervert show a marked increase (see also Chapter 2).

Such steering seems efficient, but the fact that the director and the professional are less interrelated is very problematic. This use of performance measurement only widens the natural gap between management and professionals. The director loses touch with what really happens in the professional echelons. This is a second paradox: hierarchical steering deprives management of their insight into the professional echelon, making it easier for these echelons to cause performance measurement to pervert. Hierarchical steering thus brings about its own ineffectiveness.

Why is a system nevertheless used for hierarchy purposes?

The explanation is that a director in a professional environment always finds himself in the splits described in Chapter 1. The necessary autonomy for professionals hampers steering and also hampers the obtaining of in-depth information about the activities of these professionals. At the same time there is the call for account-ability to supervisory forums (parliament, minister, supervisory board, etc.).

From this supervision perspective, a director is interested first and foremost in accountable information: information that may be helpful to him in his accounting task. This might be:

- information that has been objectified and quantified and which therefore allows comparisons over a certain time, for example;
- information that is unambiguous and does not allow too many (competing) interpretations;
- information that is highly communicable and so does not contain too much ambiguity;
- information that can be provided at the same time each year.

Systems of performance measurement appear to provide this type of information. Performance measurement thus offers the director an attractive proposition:

- he has information available about the professional process (which is always difficult in a professional environment);
- he can obtain it in a way that is efficient for him (because it does not involve high interaction costs); and
- he also has information that is very potent and functional in the director–regulator relationship.

The result is that organizations have strong incentives to maintain these systems, even though this hierarchical use accounts for the perverse effects of performance measurement. Consequently, it is tempting to see performance measurement as a form of comprehensive steering. Anyone who forms a picture of an organization on the basis of performance measurement – the thinking goes – has a comprehensive and therefore adequate picture.

Differentiation

Now it may be argued that everybody will admit that performance measurement produces a limited picture of reality. There is indeed a difference between two types of comprehensiveness. Type 1 comprehensiveness means that a director feels that performance measurement offers him rich information about reality. A director can make decisions with the help of this information. This type 1 comprehensiveness will not be found very frequently; even the director will admit that performance measurement produces a partial picture of reality.

There is also a type 2 comprehensiveness. The director admits that performance measurement presents a limited picture of reality, but feels that the cost of extra information gathering outweighs the benefits. Performance measurement does not describe the whole reality, but it provides a picture that sufficiently satisfies the director. Although this type 2 comprehensiveness is based on more subtle intentions than type 1, the result is the same. There are three explanations for type 2 comprehensiveness:

- We know from the literature about information management that different types of information compete for an actor's attention.[10] The question as to what information an actor will eventually use depends on considerations like the accessibility and unambiguous nature of the information (the more accessible and unambiguous the information, the sooner the director will use it).
- Once an actor has information, he will always ask himself during further information gathering what the marginal use of it is. He is not seeking complete information, but sufficiently satisfactory information. Once he has this, he will stop gathering new information.
- The last mechanism is reinforced by the fact that the top of an organization has a limited processing capacity. It will soon say there is an information overload.

Quantitative and qualitative information tend to compete for a director's attention. The quantitative information is easily accessible and will reach the director at some stage. The pitfall is predictable: if performance measurement provides him with a number of satisfactory images, the chances are that he will no longer seek additional information. There is a satisfactory image, so extra information gathering will not be of any marginal use. This behaviour is easily justified: the director provides outline steering and is not interested in details.

This mechanism may in turn lead to forms of strategic behaviour by the professional, which in its turn produces the paradoxical picture of the hierarchical use of performance measurement. The stronger the hierarchical steering, the more professionals will make an effort to nourish the system with information that presents a sufficiently satisfactory picture of their own performance and consequently produces less effective steering.

To summarize, performance measurement invites hierarchical application, which is exactly why it produces the perverse effects. Hierarchical steering is an incentive for perverse behaviour and deprives the director of insight into what actually happens in the primary process. Systems of performance measurement are nevertheless maintained because they provide accountable information, which is very functional for a director. This information may be dysfunctional in the director because it produces a limited or perhaps even incorrect picture of the primary process.

4 Intermezzo: performance measurement in American corporate culture

How unwise this use of performance measurement is becomes clear when I digress to a study by Philippe d'Iribarne of the use of performance measurement in American corporate culture.[11] Performance measurement is deeply rooted there, which prompts the question why performance measurement evidently survives and does not suffer the perverse effects from Chapter 2.

Irbaine points out that anyone who takes a closer look at the American use of performance measurement can conclude that it is embedded in a pattern of values characterized by features such as the following:

• The actors involved realize that goals and appraisal criteria are just an *approach* of the performance actually achieved. Actual performance is always more complex than can be laid down in the formal goals and performance indicators. Consequently, for a large part of the goals achieved there is no relation between this formal performance and the reward an employee receives.

- Performance thinking is embedded in the value of 'fairness'. The actors involved treat each other fairly. This means, for example, that the fact that a performance achieved is just an approach of reality may be a subject of discussion. This is a strong disincentive for strategic behaviour.
- Another contract value is *fairness*. This value means, among other things, that actors are prepared to change goals and performance indicators if it is reasonable to do so. After all, in a contractual relationship this is always possible after negotiation. In a hierarchical relation this is not a matter of course, because it impairs the functions of performance measurement.
- In the literature about performance measurement, reference is made to the risk that performance measurement especially appeals to feelings of fear: anyone who fails to achieve a certain performance will be punished.[12] d'Iribarne points out that the performance contract in the American culture also *binds the director*. The director also has obligations and should meet them.
- Performance thinking is accompanied by sanctions, which may be imposed when an agreed performance is not achieved. But there are procedures for the imposition of sanctions for non-performance that must *protect* a subordinate *from arbitrariness* on this point.
- Finally, it is remarkable that the parties are also aware that performance agreements have two *functions*: a 'managerial' function[13] and a political function. The latter means that parties accept that it must be made clear to outsiders what performance an organization achieves. That is the reason why the director tolerates agreements that are not always complied with, and the subordinate tolerates the performance that on paper can be a distorted picture, to his disadvantage, of the actual performance.

The essence of the above is that performance measurement is embedded in contractual values. The superior and the subordinate conclude agreements, surrounded by values like honesty, fairness and reasonableness. These values block the perverse phenomena from Chapter 2. Another part of this contract thinking is that the superior and the subordinate make a substantial investment in their interrelatedness: problems are always shared problems. Agreed goals, for example, are re-negotiable when changes occur in an organization's environment. Furthermore, director and professional are aware of the political function of performance measurement and are consequently capable of putting this system into perspective. All this is inconsistent with the hierarchical use of performance measurement.

5 Performance measurement degenerates into ritual, but maintaining it is in everybody's interest

When professionals learn how to protect themselves from hierarchical interventions, two realities are formed in an organization. First there is the reality of the primary process: professionals performing their own activities, in accordance with their own professional standards. They thus shape the primary process as they see fit, have learnt to nourish the system of performance measurement in such a way that the managerial echelon sees no reason to intervene. Apart from them there is a management echelon, which has its own reality: planning cycles, annual reports, planning and control figures, strategic memorandums, etc. This reality only has limited links with what happens in the primary process.

This situation implies that performance measurement becomes *ritualized* in an organization. First, performance measurement is deprived of its steering effect. The perverse effects force out the beneficial effects. A managerial echelon that heavily relies on performance measurement will become the victim of it. It forms pictures of achieved and desirable performance that have either little to do with reality or nothing at all. When it subsequently bases decisions or strategic choices on these pictures, they will, as a rule, lack authority and have little chance of success.

Ritualization means that the professional echelon does not fight these managerial realities but maintains them and in some cases even nourishes them. As long as both realities exist side by side and the professional has sufficient possibilities to avert hierarchical interventions, performance measurement is not threatening. It is a ritual that ensures peaceful coexistence between management and professionals. For the professionals, this situation is comfortable: the professional has sufficient degrees of freedom to shape the primary process as he thinks fit. The ritual is also comfortable for management: it has the required figures, which in many cases indicate the desired trends. The system thus nourishes the idea that everything is under control. Furthermore, the system allows limited interaction with professionals.

This may seem like a cynical picture of performance measurement, but the complaint that performance measurement is a ritual is often heard.[14] Research shows that the same system of performance measurement creates great trust among directors and great distrust among professionals.[15] Organizations invest a great deal in systems of performance measurement, but subsequently make very limited use of them.[16] Maintaining this ritual is a form of behaviour, which partly develops unintentionally and naturally: a system is dysfunctional from a professional perspective, so professionals gradually learn how to deal with it, while the managerial echelon concludes that the system is used and produces the required information. The managerial echelon may also have an interest in not using performance measurement, for example when political considerations dominate decision making.[17]

This image of performance measurement as a ritual can be valued as positive. The professional in the public sector creates a product or a service that is always a trade-off between a large number of values. A system of performance measurement measures only one or just a few of these values. The further such a system penetrates into the profession (for example, in the example of the museum director mentioned earlier, who will focus increasingly on the performance indicator that measures visitor numbers), the more steering the effect it will have (visitor numbers increase), but at the same time the more seriously it will disturb the professional trade-off.

From such a perspective, the appreciation of ritualization is positive: the perverse effect of performance measurement serves to protect the profession. Performance measurement may have some steering effect, but there are also procedural provisions to make performance accountable, the professional slightly manipulates input and throughput and there are certain forms of strategic behaviour. Thanks to this game, a sufficiently satisfactory picture develops at managerial level, and at professional level there is sufficient scope to shape the profession. A ritualized system thus creates an equilibrium between management and professionals. The perverse effects are not strong enough to harm the function of accountability and strong enough to protect the profession from excessive effects of performance measurement. This is a third explanation for the freezing of performance measurement.

On the other hand, there is a negative picture of ritualization. Performance measurement as a ritual deprives the management of insight into the actual progress of the primary process. It reduces the directors' tolerance of complexity and so is a breeding ground for bad interventions by management. Ritualization constantly confirms that the director is right: 'Often wrong, but never in doubt'.[18] The professional also benefits by a clear insight on the part of the management. When performance measurement becomes a ritual, it loses its beneficial effect. The incentives for performance disappear, which may cause the professional echelon to become introvert, perform insufficiently and insufficiently account for its performance.

6 The conclusion is that performance measurement is a layer of rock in public organizations

Performance measurement is aimed at making public organizations perform and account for their results. The result might be that the system of performance measurement forms a layer of rock in the organization between management and professionals. It deprives directors of insight into the activities performed at the bottom level of the organization. What is treacherous, however, is that the system suggests that they have a detailed insight into them. The quality of managerial interventions suffers from it.

Performance measurement particularly invites professionals to optimize their own position. This offers scope, which enterprising professionals can make good use of, but which may also degenerate into a licence for non-performance.

Part II

4 Design principles for performance measurement

1 Introduction

Apart from beneficial effects, performance measurement also has perverse effects. The chances are that the perverse effects will force out the beneficial effects in the long term. If performance measurement perverts in the long term, the inevitable question is whether and how performance measurement can be designed without these perverse effects occurring to an excessive degree. In this chapter I shall first answer this question. I shall indicate what criteria a system of performance measurement must, in my view, satisfy. These criteria are described in Section 2 and may be helpful in designing a system of performance measurement; this is why I shall refer to them as 'design principles' in the rest of this book. In Section 3, I will enter further into the difference between products and processes, which is vitally important for lively performance measurement. In Section 4, I shall indicate that process measurement, like product measurement, may produce perverse effects. I shall conclude in Section 5 with a linguistic digression about ideograms.

2 Three design principles for performance measurement

Table 4.1 below represents three design principles for performance measurement. They match the three explanations for the perverse effects of performance measurement (Chapter 2):

- performance measurement is unfair;
- performance measurement is poor;
- performance measurement is not lively.

In the following chapters I shall discuss these three design principles in more detail. The aim is not to offer a detailed 'toolbox' for

Table 4.1 Three design principles for performance measurement

Value	Matching design principle
Trust, fairness	Interaction
Content	Variety and redundance
Liveliness	Dynamic: both product and process measurement

performance measurement (it will differ from one organization to another), but to offer a number of design rules that may be helpful in designing performance measurement. Nor shall I concern myself in the following chapters with the question of how products may be defined, what valid product definitions are or how production is subsequently counted. I refer to the literature for these and similar métier-related questions and shall assume in the following chapters that an organization has a performance measurement system.

2.1 Design principle 1: interaction

An important value in performance measurement is trust. As soon as there is distrust between management and professionals, strong incentives will arise to cause the system to pervert. Such trust is not a matter of course.

- Because performance is achieved in co-production, a system of performance measurement may lead to 'unfair' appraisal, and so undermine trust in the system.
- Performance measurement may tempt the management to adopt a 'command and control' type attitude, which further undermines mutual trust between management and professionals.
- Performance measurement may tempt professionals to cause the system to pervert, for example by various forms of strategic behaviour; this, too, hardly improves mutual trust.

Trust is created only if justice is done to the fact that performance is achieved in a network of dependencies: professionals and their co-producers are mutually dependent, while the director and the professional are also mutually dependent. The latter means that performance measurement forms part of a contractual relationship between director and professional rather than a hierarchical relationship (compare the study by Philippe Irbaine). If a director does not moderate his hierarchical behaviour, performance measurement will produce perverse effects.

When a performance is achieved in a network of dependencies, it will always have to be based on *interaction* between management and professionals. The design of a system of performance measurement results from interaction, while the use of it also has a great many interaction moments. Such interaction thus concerns decisions like:

- How are products defined?
- What are the performance indicators for these products?
- How is performance measured and appraised?

Interaction has its consequences for the system of performance measurement. It stands a bigger chance of being supported by both the director and the professionals. Support leads to more *meaningful* performance measurement. Director and professionals each represent legitimate values (responsibility, professionalism). Interaction may give rise to a form of performance measurement that does maximum justice to these values. Furthermore, a system created in interaction has more owners and thus better chances of meaningful application, rather than functioning as just a bookkeeper's mechanism for settling accounts, for example.

Interaction also improves management's and professionals' trust in their mutual relations. A professional who knows that he can influence the way performance is measured and the way measured performance is dealt with, will have more trust in the director than a professional who feels subjected to performance measurement as a hierarchical intervention. Because crucial steps in performance measurement result from interaction, performance measurement is more predictable for the director as well as for professionals, since both can influence these steps; both can rely on the fact that unilateral actions are not being considered.

2.2 Design principle 2: variety and redundancy

Rendering public services is a multiple activity: several, partly conflicting criteria are at issue, constantly demanding other trade-offs. Multiplicity implies that an organization's products may be defined in various ways and so may be measured and appraised in various ways.

If this is so, the inevitable consequence is that an appraisal of professional production must always be based on a certain variety of criteria. This variety may concern product definitions, performance indicators, ways of measurement and ways of appraisal. If a product definition or a performance indicator freezes, the chances are that it will lack authority or it will nearly always lead to crooked growth in production, if an organization adjusts its behaviour.

It may be added that many organizations must render multiple accountability. Suppose a municipality must account for its performance to the central authority, its municipal council and its citizens and clients. The municipality may have to meet the different requirements of each of them, which leads to different product definitions, performance indicators and ways of measurement and appraisal. Multiple accountability may thus demand tolerance for variety. For example, different product definitions are used in different accountability relations.

One step further is taken when there is *redundancy*. Here, a variety of product definitions, performance indicators and systems of measurement and appraisal is used that overlap and may partly conflict. Redundancy has a positive connotation here, as it has in many technical systems. An airplane would be filled with double controls. This redundancy improves flight safety. Their are many other instances where redundancy does lead to increased performance of a system.[1] A variety of product definitions, performance indicators and systems of measurement and appraisal improves the quality of the measurement:

- If one, disputable product definition is chosen – in the event of a product that is difficult to define – the result may be that the performance measurement lacks authority or will lead to crooked growth.
- If it is found that, in spite of different product definitions, performance measurement always presents the same picture, this picture will consequently be more authoritative.
- If the picture proves to be different for each product definition, evidently no unambiguous picture of an organization's performance is possible and the organization's management will have to accept this for a fact.

It should be pointed out, however, that there are limits to variety and redundance because a system of performance measurement can only fulfil its functions when there is a certain consistency and stability. Comparison, appraisal and reward may be hampered if there is a high tolerance of variety and redundance. The aim is to strike a balance between consistency and stability on the one hand and variety and redundance on the other hand. Here, too, there is a tendency to go to extremes. From the perspective of accountability, to stability and consistency; from the perspective of professionalism, to extreme variety.

2.3 Design principle 3: dynamic

It is typical of the two preceding design principles that they stay within the paradigm of performance measurement on the level of products: an authority provides products and services and should be evaluated by its output. Performance measurement may also focus on the *professional process of achieving* the performance.

It is important for performance measurement to be lively: it must be able to deal with and do justice to the dynamic occurring in the generation of products and services. This dynamic may occur on the level of *products*: organizations develop new products or arrive at a different composition of their product package. Dynamic will also occur on the level of the *processes* of generating a product. What efforts does an organization make, how innovative is it, how does it deal with a constantly changing environment, what activities does it prioritize, how does it maintain relations with third parties that may influence its performance?

Performance measurement merely focusing on products is blind to dynamic in these processes and may degenerate into a dead activity. While a great deal of dynamic occurs in the organization, the focus continues to be on production, which – as I said earlier – always presents a limited picture of performance. Mere product measurement does no justice to an organization that maintains its production level under difficult circumstances, thanks to all sorts of innovations in the process of product generation.

This constitutes a third design principle: performance measurement should be lively and should for that reason make the dynamic visible in (1) product development and in (2) the process of generating these products. In Chapter 7, I shall indicate that performance measurement also becomes lively by using the tension between product measurement and process measurement. To explain this design principle further, I shall first discuss the difference between product and process in more detail.

3 Product and process

Table 4.2 below represents the differences between performance measurement focusing on products and performance measurement focusing on processes.[2] When a university's educational performance must be appraised, products play a role (the number of master's

Table 4.2 Performance measurement of products and processes

Product-oriented performance measurement	Process-oriented performance measurement
Result	Throughput
Low tolerance of more than one standard	High tolerance of the use of more standards
Appraisal by an expert	Dialogue between professionals
'Long distance' methods	'Local' methods
External reviewer	Internal reviewer
Ex post checks	'Real time' picture
All functions, including sanctions	Strong accent on learning function
Nouns	Verbs
'Demystification'	Surprise
Mutual trust low	Mutual trust high

degrees, for example), but processes as well. Questions about the quality of the learning materials, the use of information and communication technology in the programme and the relation between theory and practice material are hardly considered from a product perspective, although they are of the utmost importance for the educational process.

Besides, more *standards* are possible for the same performance. Suppose a reviewer concludes that the learning material looks unorganized: students must study a lot of readers containing articles that show little coherence. The appraisal of it may be negative: the readers are difficult to study, students opting for independent study (without teacher guidance) will have trouble assimilating the subject matter, no comprehensive survey of the discipline is presented, etc. Another standard is possible, however. The learning style of the present generation of students differs from that of preceding generations. It has become much more fragmented under the influence of the Internet, among other things; today's student is a 'homo zappiens'.[3] The reader fits this learning style and invites students to find out the connections between the articles themselves, to discover a leitmotiv themselves and to use other sources of information for this purpose, including the Internet in particular, of course. Both standards are legitimate. In product measurement more standards can be applied (see the design principle of variety), but tolerance of it is more limited than in process measurement, given the functions of product measurement (which require some stability).

Process measurement does not aim to find an absolute standard. It is far more important that the actors concerned admit that more standards are possible and enter into a dialogue about it with each other. In a question-and-answer game between professionals, joint pictures of the performance of the organization are created. Consensus about these pictures might develop among the actors concerned. When these pictures become lodged in the organization, it will subsequently achieve better performance. If such consensus does not emerge and there is dissension, this is a fact to be respected. Evidently, both professional appraisals of the same reality are possible. The dialogue will continue, which at least means that the supporters of both pictures will constantly have to give account. The director also has a role to play. As facilitator, he organizes the dialogue between the professionals, hears the results of it, appraises and takes a decision.

Anyone looking at the professional process in such a way tends to use *'local' appraisal mechanisms*. He does not need a generally applicable appraisal system, but tends to use methods that fit the specific circumstances of the organization in question, its profession and the services it offers. A generic appraisal system with aggregated production targets will do no justice to it in most cases. Given the above, an internal reviewer will, as a rule, be best able to form a rich picture about the process.

An attitude of a certain surprise will often fit process measurement. Anyone who penetrates the profession may become impressed by its complexity and richness. The dialogue with professionals tends to reveal their 'tacit knowledge', which then produces a richer dialogue and richer pictures. Process measurement uses verbs. The reviewer is not so much interested in master's degrees, official police reports and appraisals, but in teaching, promoting safety and trading-off interests. The product approach is based rather on an attitude of demystification. There is a complex and hard-to-understand primary process, which can be described and understood thanks to the measurement of products.

Process measurement is thus a lively and 'ongoing' process. By interacting, management and professionals frequently form pictures of the performance achieved. An internal reviewer is close to the professional process and is therefore able to form much more 'ongoing' and 'real time' pictures of, and comment, on performance than the external reviewer, who appraises performance ex post.

This form of performance measurement may have a steering effect because the reviewer, the director and professionals learn about the performance, about the standards for the performance and about possible improvements. Consequently, *learning* is the aim of process measurement. As soon as it developed into a tool to sanction professionals, the mechanism from Table 2.1 would take effect: the stronger the steering, the less effective performance measurement. Furthermore, when more standards for production are possible, sanctioning is difficult. If the accent is on learning rather than sanctioning, trust may arise between the reviewer and the professionals; trust is a *sine qua non* for the proper functioning of process measurement.

4 The perverse effects of process measurement

It would now appear that the product approach simply cannot compare with the process approach, but I shall demonstrate in Chapter 7 that it is nevertheless meaningful. Those who exclusively opt for a product approach will in the long term create the perverse effects from Chapter 2. The process approach does not substitute it, but supplements the product approach and makes it lively. If performance measurement exclusively concerned processes, it would also result in perverse effects.

Process measurement is based on the idea that interaction between professionals produces rich or richer pictures about performance. These pictures become embedded among professionals and will therefore cause change in their behaviour. However, the assumption underlying process measurement – that professionals are able to arrive at a picture about performance by interacting – is contestable for several reasons:[4]

- Professional relations tend to be marked by interdependence and non-intervention: a professional has little to do with the work of other professionals and in exchange for it he can expect these other professionals not to meddle with his work. They are thus capable of peaceful coexistence. When, for example, an internal reviewer appraises professional activities on the basis of 'local methods', the chances are that the non-intervention principle will apply.
- In interaction processes, professionals will show a strong inclination to advocate or even defend issues. This means that, by interacting with other people, they will go to great lengths to defend their own performance. Problems are easily externalized: they do not seek the causes of problems in their own behaviour, but in that of others. The dialogue between professionals is typical of process measurement (versus appraisal by an expert, see Table 4.2). Professionals may also use dialogue to generate a large number of fallacies in order to justify non-performance. Combined with the non-intervention principle, it will be fruitless.

- Professionals may have little eye for possibilities for innovation. One example here is Mintzberg's well-known 'pigeonholing': professionals have a strong tendency to assign new developments to existing categories.[5]

Process measurement may thus pervert. After some time it only creates fallacies and occasional arguments. An internal reviewer with his 'local methods' may be so close to the organization to be appraised that adequate appraisal is impossible. The features of process measurement – dialogue, learning, 'high trust' – become a justification to abandon appraisal. In course of time, dependencies will be operative and there will be a strong incentive for the internal reviewer to abandon his critical attitude towards his fellow professional. He may need this fellow professional in the future; such dependence does not benefit from critical appraisal. So here, too, the picture is ambiguous. This results in the same type of question as that raised in the discussion of product measurement: how to deal with this ambiguity? See Chapter 7 for a further discussion of this issue.

5 Performance measurement as an ideogram

To conclude this chapter, I would like to digress into the field of language. The literature about performance measurement contains many pleas for performance measurement, consisting of building blocks like:

- it is necessary to develop *consistent* product definitions;
- performance measurement is a form of *comprehensive* steering, all products of an organization must be included in the system;
- performance indicators must be *complete*.

Concepts like 'comprehensive', 'consistent' and 'complete' always sound good in the managerial and consulting jargon. In rhetoric, such concepts are called *ideograms*.[6] An ideogram has three characteristics:

- An ideogram represents a collective, normative obligation. Everybody is in favour of comprehensiveness, consistency and a complete approach.
- Ideograms tend to justify disputable or harmful phenomena. A certain policy may be ineffective or inefficient, but they are justified by raising the defence of the comprehensive, consistent and complete nature of this policy.
- An ideogram is always slightly ambiguous and has no fixed meaning. The meaning of the concepts may vary. Such a concept will therefore survive.

In this and the preceding chapters I have demonstrated that comprehensiveness and consistency are problematic in performance measurement. Comprehensive performance measurement is a strong incentive for perverting behaviour. Consistency does no justice to the multiple character of public products; tolerating variety is far more attractive. In Chapter 6 I shall discuss the idea of completeness. The recommendation there will be not to seek completeness.

These concepts have great rhetorical force, however; they reduce a complex reality to something that is easily surveyable and understandable. They continue to resurface due to their rhetorical force and produce all sorts of negative effects. These concepts survive because they are slightly ambiguous. When comprehensiveness, consistency and completeness are eventually found to be dysfunctional, this will nevertheless not easily bring pleas for partial performance measurement, based on inconsistent product definitions. Ideograms like comprehensiveness, consistency and completeness are powerful concepts, but they are also multi-interpretable. They will be amended slightly and can then work again. In other words, ideograms hamper an organization's learning by and block the road to improvement of performance measurement. This is why ideograms are very harmful. It is necessary to unmask concepts as ideograms, thus making room for a more intelligent use of performance measurement.

5   Trust and interaction

1 Introduction

Performance measurement may widen the gap between management and professionals, as was shown in Chapter 3; it invites 'command and control' and minimization of mutual interaction. This is the reason why interaction should be ensured between management and professionals at a number of key moments in the performance measurement process. Interaction improves the confidence they have in each other and in the system of performance measurement.

Of course, interaction plays a role in the design of a performance measurement system. Professionals may be invited to indicate what good product definitions are and by what definitions they wish to be appraised. When management and professionals subsequently arrive at product definitions and performance indicators in mutual consultation, there is a growing chance that these will find support and can therefore fulfil their functions.

Once a system exists, interaction will also play an important role in the *use* of it. Decision making about the following subjects requires some form of interaction.

- What are the functions of performance measurement and for what forums are the results of performance measurement meant? The design principle of interaction here means that neither management nor professionals may unilaterally change the functions or forums of performance measurement. Once performance measurement has a function and a forum, both management and professionals must be able to trust that deviating from it requires some form of consultation. Unilateral accumulation of functions and/or forums may also harm trust in the system (Section 2).
- What is the relation between a professional's production on the one hand and its appraisal by the director on the other hand? Section 3 indicates that appraisal should always come about in

interaction between management and professionals. If it does not
– the director appraises without consultation – performance
measurement will pervert drastically.

These two effects of the principle of interaction will particularly
improve professionals' confidence in performance measurement. In
addition, there are two effects that improve directors' confidence in
performance measurement:

* Professional units tend to have their own forms of performance
  measurement, notably in layered organizations. From the director's
  perspective, the risk is that this decentralized performance
  measurement is inconsistent with central performance measurement. The design principle of interaction means that management
  and professional units should make agreements about the scope
  for decentralized performance measurement (Section 4). This
  leads to an intermezzo about the 'boundary spanner', the actor
  operating on the boundary between the managerial and the
  professional system (Section 5).
* Finally, performance is stated by the professional unit. An important question is whether the performance reported is consistent
  with reality. From a management's perspective, certain checks are
  desirable. The most effective one is a 'soft' check, performed
  interactively (Section 6).

2 Clarity about functions and forums; no unilateral transformation of function and/or forum

The need for agreements about functions and forums

As I said earlier, accountability in many cases concerns multiple
activities. Furthermore, many organizations are accountable to several
forums. One of the first key preconditions for a trustful relationship is
the recognition that performance indicators always present partial
information. The picture will always depend partly on the *function*
that performance measurement fulfils (transparency, learning,
appraisal, sanctioning or comparing) and on the forum for which
performance measurement is meant.

It is therefore necessary for management and professionals to make
agreements about the *functions* of the figures and about the *forums*
for which they are meant.[1] If they fail to do so, there is a good chance
that a system will pervert. It will do so in the first place because
profound distrust may grow among the professionals about the way

performance measurement will be used, which will nearly always be an incentive to cause the system to pervert.

For a number of years now in the Netherlands, the school inspectorate's performance figures of secondary schools have been published by the press.[2] This suggests that these schools are mutually comparable (a cautionary note stating that this is not so usually accompanies such publications). Suppose a marketing organization copied this tradition and used the figures to set a 'benchmark', allowing parents to make a better-founded choice of school. A function (benchmark) and a forum (parents) would then be added to the original function (learning, appraisal) and the original forum (the inspectorate). There is every chance that this will produce two negative consequences. First, it will lead to various forms of perverse behaviour by schools because the choice made by parents is vital to a school's survival (see the 'counselling out' strategy in the American educational system, Chapter 2; or schools will sacrifice a good educational climate). Secondly, the benchmark function becomes so dominant that the figures can no longer fulfil the learning and appraisal functions in the relation between the inspectorate and individual schools. Consequently, one additional agreement is that neither management nor professionals can unilaterally decide to change either functions or forums. This creates predictability and thus improves trust in the system and mutual trust between management and professionals.

When there are no clear agreements about functions and forums, there is a strong temptation to use performance measurement for a multitude of functions and forums. Such an accumulation of functions will trigger the following mechanism:

- every function and every forum creates its own beneficial effects;
- every function and every forum creates its own perverse effects;
- perverse effects eventually force out the beneficial effects;
- in time, an accumulation of functions and/or forums will therefore cause an accumulation of perverse behaviour.

A system that must fulfil a large number of functions simultaneously tends to collapse under its own complexity. The definition of products alone will be highly problematic, given the multiple character of public performance. For example, it will be almost impossible to define a 'scientific article' so that it can be used in the allocation model of a university (result: the definition will have to fit the various disciplines within the university), as an international 'benchmark' (result: the definition will have to match the standards in a specific discipline) and as a 'hands-on' management tool (result: it will have to fit the specific circumstances of a professional unit).

So unambiguous definitions will easily cause problems when there is an accumulation of functions or forums. They simply do not match the various functions or forums and lead to endless definitional exercises. If, instead, a variety of product definitions is tolerated, an accumulation of functions and forums will lead to an accumulation of product definitions, which partly overlap or may even be mutually conflicting. This may cause problems, too. Many definitions with considerable overlap will at some stage harm the system. See Chapter 6 about the need for, and constraints posed by, variety.

These agreements would seem obvious, given the examples, but the temptation to accumulate functions and forums may be great. The explanation is a simple one. The further a director is removed from the primary process, the more his insight into this primary process decreases and, consequently, so does his tolerance of the complexity and multiplicity of this process. A need for unambiguous figures arises and, consequently, there is less appreciation of the fact that one performance can be quantified in several ways.

Obscurity about functions and forums produces perverse effects

A related phenomenon is *obscurity* about the function of figures. Such obscurity again invites perverting behaviour. For instance, during a certain period there is considerable political interest in the judiciary. The court is asked in a particular year to state the number of press contacts per year. It is unclear why this is desirable and what meaning the ministry might attach to it. This lack of clarity about the function is one reason to take a critical look at the 'product' press contact. Is there a press contact when a reporter phones to enquire about the time of a hearing? Or when a press release has been issued? Or only when a reporter is allowed an interview about the nature of the court's activities? The lack of clarity about the function of the figure and about the product definition poses a risk from the perspective of the court in question (at least, a lot of hassle caused by the ministry). This risk is easy to limit by making an agreement with the court in the neighbouring district about the figure to be provided. 'Don't count but call' (the neighbour court), as the saying goes.

This again shows the futility of the search for a comprehensive system (in the sense of being suitable for all functions and forums). The opposite is a more moderate stance: limited functions for a limited number of forums. For the professional, this creates the confidence that the figures have limited significance, which does justice to the complexity of his primary process. This will subsequently improve trust between management and professionals and thus have a moderating effect on perverting behaviour.

3 Indirect linkage of production, appraisal and reward

When professional production is known, a direct or indirect link can be made between production, appraisal and the (positive or negative) reward based on it. A direct link means that in the event of a given production, the appraisal and/or reward is 'self-executing'.

- A police force's performance indicator is the number of official police reports made. Every division should produce a predetermined number of official reports per officer per year. Production will be calculated at the end of the year. Force command indicates that the divisional commanders failing to meet the pre-arranged standard will face problems; the commander with the lowest score will lose his post.
- A university's performance indicator is the number of scientific articles published. A sum of money is paid for each published article. A faculty's research budget in a budget year depends on the number of articles published in the previous year multiplied by the price per article.

In both situations, a certain production automatically leads to a certain appraisal: the loss or retainment of the post or a certain budget amount.

The advantage of a direct link is that it may be a strong incentive to perform. A direct link may be particularly useful when an organization has lost all orientation towards output and is wholly internally oriented (throughput-oriented). It may stimulate an organization to become result-oriented again.

However, a direct link may also be a strong incentive for the perverse effects from Chapter 2. First, because a direct link will be experienced as 'unfair' in the event of co-production, when there is no causal relationship between effort and performance or when the quality of the performance is difficult to define. Secondly, when the appraisal concerns the core values of an individual or organization. Retaining a post or the availability of funds sufficient to perform core tasks are of vital importance for those concerned and justify perverting behaviour.

A direct link may also have negative consequences for a director. Once there is a direct link, the director is tied to it. He will be obliged to remove the commander in question from office and he will be obliged to allocate the promised funds to a faculty. This may make the director the prisoner of his own system. One of the better commanders may turn out to score poorly or a strategically important faculty publishes so little that it will have to abandon part of its research. It should be pointed out, however, that they will probably oppose the direct link because the poorly performing divisional commander's or faculty's core values are affected. If they succeed, the direct link will cause the director loss of face. A direct link might seem to be a form of powerful management, but it frequently leads to efforts to undo the consequences.

The need for an indirect link

When there is an indirect link between production, appraisal and reward, the appraisal and reward to which a certain production will lead are also indicated in advance. The link between these three is not 'self-executing', however. Establishing production, appraisal and sanctioning are separate activities; there is always room for manoeuvre between these three activities. Appraisal is not given until management and professionals have exchanged views about performance. If output is low, it may be asked what caused it. Was it due to sloppy management, to carefully considered professional choices of other priorities or to external circumstances? Given the picture that the director has, he will then give an appraisal. For the professional, this means that he still has some room for manoeuvre. The axe does not fall as soon as production has been established. The professional may still point out practical causes for lagging production.

Indirect links are necessary because they moderate perverse behaviour, since there is *scope* for the professional to influence appraisal after performance. This adds to his trust in the system and in the director. Suppose production is substantially lower than planned due to the behaviour of the professional's co-producers, or that a low reward would affect the professional organization's core values. Indirect linkage always leaves room to discuss this item with management, which may lead to moderation of the appraisal.

Risks of indirect linkage

Indirect links are necessary, but also carry major risks:

- They might tempt a director to take arbitrary measures. A certain reward per product has been agreed in advance, but the director

may withdraw from it afterwards thanks to the indirect link. For the professional, this means that the consequences of his performance become unpredictable.
• They may be a reason for a professional to avoid the steering effect of performance measurement. Indirect linkage always offers the poorly performing and opportunist professional a possibility to avoid the consequences.

How can these risks be prevented? The answer is: by agreeing a number of clear *rules of the game* about the *process* from establishing performance to appraisal. Suppose, for example, that in this process a simple rule of the game applies: 'Management shall consult with professionals about performance and then appraise performance; if managerial appraisal differs from the appraisal by professionals, arguments shall be presented'.

Such a rule of the game 'forces' the director to listen to a professional when giving his appraisal. He has the freedom, however, to deviate from the professional's image of performance, but is obliged to put forward arguments in that case. The idea is that this rule of the game, particularly the obligation to put forward arguments, on the one hand reduces the risk of managerial arbitrariness. The rule of the game on the other hand demands explicit appraisal, reducing the risks of professional opportunism.

This creates an arrangement with the following characteristics:

• No direct link will be made.
• Instead, linkage will be indirect, allowing both director and professional room for manoeuvre in giving an appraisal and fixing the reward. This room is necessary because performance measurement will never do full justice to professional activities.
• The risk of indirect linkage is that it may lead to managerial arbitrariness and professional opportunism.
• A clear procedure is therefore agreed, from the establishment of production, through appraisal, to fixing the reward. This procedure moderates the risks of a soft link.

It is worth noting, however, that the aim of all this is a certain moderation of performance measurement. This may also be reached in a different way, for example by also tolerating other systems of appraisal in addition to performance measurement. For example, if only part of the budget is made dependent on performance measurement, there is a form of moderation and a direct link will cause fewer problems. See Chapter 6 about this.

Process arrangements

The idea of process arrangements will return when the design principles are discussed in more detail, which is why I will enter into this issue here briefly. This way of thinking is rooted in the literature about process management.[3] The underlying idea is that, when there is a particular problem, it is often either impossible or undesirable for a director:

- to take a content-related decision,
- ex ante,
- and subsequently to enforce compliance with it.

If this is the case, an alternative to enforcement as far as content is concerned is that management invests in a *process* to reach a decision and subsequently implement it. So no content, but process; no command and control, but process.

Applying this to the link between performance, appraisal and reward, it is unwise to indicate ex ante, in precise terms, how this link will be made and also impose this intended link as binding (unless the professional is granted scope in some other way). The alternative is indirect linkage and a specified *process of* linkage. These and similar process arrangements bring the following advantages.

- They are a form of 'mild' compulsion. The process agreement demands maximum prudence of appraisal, at the same time allowing scope to both director and professional.
- They are fair: the professional has a fair chance of influencing the director's appraisal; the director is forced to argue his decisions.
- They offer an opportunity to learn; by interacting, both director and professional can learn from each other about the nature of the performance.
- They add to the authority of the eventual decision; obedience to the rules of the game forces director and professional to explicitly explain their arguments to each other. If relations between director and professional are normal, this will add to the authority of the eventual decision.
- They contribute to the predictability of the decision making. The advantage of a direct link is that decision making is predictable. This is not so if the link is indirect, but rules of the game nevertheless offer a certain predictability. A professional knows how decisions about appraisal and reward are made, knows that he has a fair chance in this process, but also knows that a consistent decision will be taken about his performance.

A process agreement should thus moderate the disadvantages of indirect linkage as much as possible: no arbitrariness or opportunism, but prudent behaviour. This also prevents a constant pendulum between direct and indirect linkage.

4 Process arrangements about the level from which the incentive is dampened and about the tolerance of a decentralized incentive structure

An important question in the design of performance measurement is down to what level the incentive provided by performance measurement must be perceptible. Suppose a product is defined by a central managerial echelon, indicating that a reward will follow if a certain production is realized. This financial incentive might then be passed on to a decentralized echelon, which in turn passes on the incentive to a lower echelon. Can this incentive then be passed on to an individual professional? This individual would then know exactly what products produce what financial reward: if a certain production of official police reports, appraisals, rulings, publications and suchlike is achieved, he might be able to calculate how much money he generates for the organization.

Tolerance of dampening the incentive and of a decentralized incentive structure: a dilemma

The answer to this question also requires differentiation. On the one hand, the literature frequently warns against translating financial incentives to the level of individual employees.[4]

First, performance measurement may produce perverse effects and these effects will be greatest when the incentive is placed on the level of the individual. When a production target is imposed on the lowest level in the organization – the individual professional – this means that all units in the organization are subjected to these perverting effects. They will therefore manifest themselves very strongly.

Secondly, much of the literature points out that performance indicators that are perceptible on the level of the individual tend to be threatening to the individual professional. This gives performance measurement a negative connotation, which increases the temptation to pervert the system.

This presents one of the first pictures: performance measurement, translated to the individual level, will cause the system to pervert to an extreme degree. The conclusion is that the incentive should be dampened somewhere between the central managerial echelon and the individual professional.

On the other hand, the incentive may be dampened so severely that the benefit of performance measurement will get lost. This is a frequent phenomenon in organizations and it presents a second picture:

- a performance measurement system is introduced,
- it then has to be translated through a number of levels,
- the incentive is dampened on one or more of these levels,
- causing it to be no longer perceptible on the level where performance must be achieved.

Closely linked with this problem is the phenomenon that a (decentralized) professional unit may develop its own incentive structure, which may differ from the incentive structure included in the (central) system of performance measurement. On the one hand, this may be undesirable: two conflicting incentive structures are used. The steering effect of performance measurement may thus get lost. On the other hand, a professional unit may have sound arguments for dampening particular central incentives, since these may have the above-mentioned perverting effect: they force out attention for quality, innovation and system responsibility, for example. This may also be formulated in positive terms: developing a decentralized incentive structure may do justice to the special circumstances particular to the decentralized unit. Performance measurement may thus have its beneficial effects.

Process arrangements

Here, too, it is important that organizations should draw up process arrangements, based on the following considerations:

- There are two dilemmas: allowing incentives to make themselves felt everywhere versus dampening incentives, and prohibiting a decentralized incentive structure versus tolerating a decentralized incentive structure.
- It is difficult and unwise for a management to give an ex ante and binding indication as to the shape of the decentralized incentive structure.
- Instead, a process arrangement is made: the rule of the game then is that the professional unit shows management how and where it dampens the incentives and where it deviates from the central model, stating its arguments.

- Management may then give an argued appraisal.
- Process arrangements can also be made about the 'burden of proof'. The agreement may be, for example, that management will in principle accept the professional unit's line of reasoning, unless it finds it clearly incorrect or unreasonable. A test of reasonableness of the arguments is then conducted and the burden of proof to deviate from it rests with the management. The agreement may, of course, also be that the professional unit carries the burden of proof to present arguments for deviating from the views of the management.

I shall now illustrate this by paying attention to the role of the 'boundary spanner'.

5 Intermezzo: the importance of the boundary spanner between management and profession

Performance measurement should take place in the area of tension formed by the complexity of the profession and the need for accountability. An important task facing a director is that performance measurement should be meaningful (lively, content-based) for professionals. The reverse is true as well. The important task facing a professional is to answer for his performance in a way that is meaningful for the director. The content of the account given must match the rationality of the managerial process. For example, it must be possible to establish a clear link between the account given and an organization's strategy, or the account given must make clear the critical developments within the profession.

In many cases, performance measurement initiated by the managerial echelon lacks meaning. However, the opposite picture often applies as well: professionals answer for their performance in language and in pictures matching the rationality of the profession rather than the rationality of the director. Such an account will then lack meaning for the director.

This is not surprising, however: condensing information about the profession in a number of dominant pictures, meaningful for the managerial echelon, is a skill not always mastered by the professional echelon, since it requires knowledge of the processes that play a part on the managerial level.

When accountability from the professional system requires insight into the managerial system, and interventions by the management require insight into the professional system, the question who has sufficient knowledge of both systems becomes an interesting one.

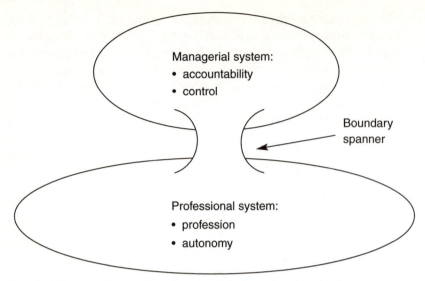

Figure 5.1 Trust and interaction: the role of the boundary spanner

The solution is that in every organization, somewhere between the managerial echelon and the individual professional, there is nearly always a player who participates in the managerial game as well as having profound knowledge of the profession. This player is referred to as the 'boundary spanner'. It is vitally important for the effect of performance measurement to identify this 'boundary spanner' (Figure 5.1). He is sufficiently close to the professional process to influence it and sufficiently close to the managerial echelon to understand the interests of this echelon and do justice to them.

In many cases, this 'boundary spanner' is thus best able to make the trade-off between managerial and professional interests. He can translate managerial interventions to the professional echelon and translate professional experiences and performance to the managerial echelon. The boundary spanner must be allowed sufficient scope to do so, by both management and professionals.

- He needs sufficient scope to make 'trade-offs' at the professional level between production on the one hand and values like innovation and system responsibility on the other. This may mean that particular individuals are brought in to achieve the unit's production, while others are given the opportunity to develop innovation or carry system responsibility.
- He needs scope to make central incentives meaningful and significant for professionals. An incentive in a police organization that

rewards official police reports has little meaning. If it is translated to the individual professional, the chances are that many bagatelle police reports will be written. The 'boundary spanner' can make this incentive meaningful by translating it into goals matching the specific circumstances of the relevant professional unit. Of course, this is possible only if he is allowed scope for it.

- He needs scope to contribute to the account given by the management. The professionals will have to offer him this scope, for example, in the form of willingness to achieve performance with high managerial priority (and, possibly, low professional priority).

First and foremost, it is the boundary spanner who can answer the question what a desirable decentralized incentive structure is. This is because the answer must on the one hand reckon with the managerial interest that performance measurement must have a stimulating effect, whilst on the other hand justice must be done to a professional unit's specific characteristics.

If a boundary spanner has sufficient scope, he can convert a central incentive structure into a structure that fits the characteristics of the decentralized, professional organization. Something similar applies to the question at how low a level in the organization an incentive must be perceptible; this question can best be answered by the boundary spanner. This also requires scope for the boundary spanner. If he has to deal with employees whose performance is poor, he may make the incentive felt at a lower level than if he has to deal with employees who are already strongly driven by their own interests. The boundary spanner makes his choice and may submit it to management, who will then decide.

6 Process arrangements about checks

When professional organizations are rewarded on the basis of performance, this means that their products are worth money. This may occasion all sorts of strategic behaviour by the professional part of the organization. In many cases, the system of performance measurement offers scope for it. The product definitions may be insufficiently refined or further refinement of product definitions is reasonably impossible.

> Universities and schools of professional education provide 'unreliable' figures about their number of graduates. These figures, known as success rates, are calculated in various ways. (. . .) Some courses do not include the students that abandon their studies

during the first year in their success rate; others do. One faculty includes in its calculations entrants holding a certificate of Higher Professional Education, who are allowed to skip the first year at university. This raises their first-year success rate above that of other courses. Some courses only report the average length of study of their graduates, thus ignoring drop-outs. (. . .). The Association of Universities in the Netherlands (VSNU) has a guideline for the calculation of success rates (. . .). VSNU says it appreciates that 'faculties find it difficult to follow that guideline (. . .). They have to deal with students registered for two courses but only paying tuition fees for one, or with students that hardly show up or do not show up at all and so drop out' (those known as ghost registrants, causing the success rate to be lower, without the faculty being able to do anything about it, HdB).[5]

There may be a strong incentive to report the highest possible production, particularly when performance is worth money. Every system offers some room for this: the question whether a product comes within the product definitions of the system can never be answered fully ex ante.

How should these problems be dealt with? First and foremost, particular forms of unilateral checks by management can be beneficial. At my own university, a hard copy of every publication entered must be sent to the Executive Board. This allows the Board to check whether publications have actually been produced and properly classified by the relevant faculty. The checks thus made possible are not without success, as an evaluation shows. For example, external reports are only rewarded if they have a minimum length. Checks prevent this minimum length being reached only by a certain layout of the reports.[6] Such a check can be used to filter out evident inaccuracies from the production reported.

Most of the checks will be interactive, however. This is necessary because one definition of a product may cover entirely different realities. In the first example:

- Students are not sure about their choice of study, they register for a number of studies at once, but follow only one or, at most, two. Some courses are prone to these double registrations (they have many 'ghost registrants'), others hardly see them or do not see them at all.
- Universities are inventive. They design all sorts of fast tracks for Higher Professional Education students, each with a different form and length.

It is not easy to deal with this underlying complexity. If further refinement is impossible, stricter checks on the production achieved are rather pointless. As long as the same product definitions may cover different realities, only limited checks are possible, since strict adherence to particular product definitions will lead to evident injustice. Such strict adherence would seriously harm a system's legitimacy, and thus – given the possibilities to pervert the system – also harm its effectiveness. This again leads to one of the many paradoxes of performance measurement: strict adherence to formal product definitions harms the legitimacy of the system. How then should we deal with the fact that refinement and checks encounter natural boundaries, whilst at the same time large-scale widening of product definitions should be prevented?

The answer to this question is that most of the check is also an interactive process. This means that management and professionals jointly form a picture of the variety of products covered by the same product definition. They can then form a joint picture of the extent to which they will tolerate or not tolerate this.

The primary aim of such a check is to learn about the variety of products. A management may subsequently decide about the extent to which this variety will be tolerated and whether product definitions may need to be reviewed. New rules of the game can be agreed for forming this joint picture and the ensuing decision making. The core of it will always be:

- by interaction, management and professionals form a picture of the products suggested for appraisal and about how these relate to the formal product definitions;
- they then form a picture about which products reasonably come within the product definition and which do not;
- they make an agreement about how they will deal in the future with products that do not come within the product definition.

Process arrangements like these are an incentive to reach joint agreements (they reduce the risk of unilateral managerial decision making); joint agreements increase the legitimacy of the system of performance measurement. If there is no such check, the variety covered by a product definition may increase without the parties concerned noticing it. If this variety becomes visible later – see the above quotation about the success rates of universities – the impression of mismanagement will easily be created. Of course, the parties should be selective in designing these checks: checks should be cost effective. Part of the process arrangements might be that parties indicate for what product definitions they wish to examine the underlying variety.

6 Content and variety

1 Introduction

Performance measurement might easily be poor and does not become meaningful until a performance is viewed from several perspectives, because this is how justice is done to the multiplicity of the performance. One of the first effects of this design principle was mentioned in Chapter 1: a public performance must always be identified by several indicators. If we assume that performance is mapped by more than one indicator, there will be three additional effects of the design principle of variety:

- Once a performance has been mapped, then the question is who is allowed to attach a meaning to the figures: who has the 'meaning-making rights'? Variety means that there is no monopoly of meaning giving (Section 2).
- The use of different product definitions is necessary, but for an organization to tolerate competing product definitions is another step. This means that the same performance can be made visible in different, competing ways. This will be the subject of Section 3.
- Finally, variety is also opposed to comprehensiveness. Comprehensiveness means that every performance by an organization is measured and therefore included in a comprehensive system of performance measurement. The principle of variety means that a distinction is made between various types of performance and that an organization tolerates each of these different types to play a role (or no role, in some cases) in the system of performance measurement (Section 4).

2 Meaning giving: no monopoly on the 'meaning-making rights'

An important question in performance measurement is what meaning must be assigned to the figures and, consequently, who has the 'meaning-making rights':[1] who gives meaning to the figures? To illustrate the importance of this question, here are a number of figures from the planning and control cycle of the Ministry of Justice (Table 6.1).[2] What meaning should be given to these figures?

The figures show how many acts of violence are committed against staff in remand centres (RCs) and what sanctions the management of the remand centres imposes on the inmates. These sanctions have a rising degree of compulsion: solitary confinement, placement in an isolation cell or a placement in a national solitary confinement department.

Suppose violence in prisons is a matter of grave concern to the Minister of Justice and that this item is also high on the agenda of the Lower House of Parliament. The minister is then faced with these figures and must form an appraisal about the 'performance' of these remand centres. Which RC is doing well as regards the curbing of violence and which RC shows a poor performance? The following interpretations of the above figures are possible (each of these meanings *may* be construed. Whether they are correct is not the issue here).

Meaning 1

'A' has a great deal of violence and therefore frequently uses sanctions; B has less violence and, consequently, a lower use of sanctions. C has less violence *because* it applies more sanctions. This meaning may be construed by someone who only has these figures available. They do not lead to conclusions about the question which RC performs better, except the conclusion that an RC that applies sanctions relatively soon will have fewer acts of violence. The question remains whether this conclusion is correct.

Table 6.1 Acts of violence against staff and sanctions within three remand centres

| | Remand centre | | |
	A	B	C
Acts of violence against staff	28	2	8
– per 100 cells occupied	11	3.7	2.8
Solitary confinements	68	15	461
– per 100 cells occupied	26.6	27.5	161.1
Placement in isolation cell	35	12	257
– per 100 cells occupied	13.7	22.0	89.8
Placement in national solitary confinement department	5.0	1.0	0
– per 100 cells occupied	2.0	1.8	0

Meaning 2

RCs 'B' and 'C' have been designated as RCs with an austere regime. This means that many inmates are kept in cells and that consequently there are fewer acts of violence. RC 'A' has a standard regime and therefore more acts of violence.

This meaning may be construed by the person who has the above figures available and has information about the regime in the institutions. This information is easy to obtain. The conclusion is that only 'B' and 'C' are comparable. There is not much difference between the two institutions as regards acts of violence; RC 'C' does have a great many more sanctions. 'B' therefore shows a better performance.

Meaning 3

RC 'A' has many acts of violence and imposes many sanctions. However, its inmates lodge many written complaints against the sanctions. Far fewer written complaints are lodged in RCs 'B' and 'C'. The conclusion is that the management of RC 'A' is easily inclined to feel that particular behaviour by inmates constitutes an act of violence. There is more tolerance in RCs 'B' and 'C'.

This meaning may be construed by the person who has the above figures available and also has additional information about the number of written complaints. This information, too, is still fairly easy to obtain. The conclusion is already becoming more diffuse: the figures say something about how the management defines particular behaviour by inmates and not only about this behaviour itself.

Meaning 4

The policy in RCs 'A' and 'B' is that placements are not applied frequently, but they are long. The idea is that this has the most deterring effect. RC 'C' has not got this philosophy. The result is that the figures not only show the number of acts of violence, but also reflect the policy of the RC concerned. The same figure thus has two meanings, which makes it difficult to draw a conclusion.

Meaning 5

RCs 'A' and 'B' are more decentralized than C. This means that the head of a unit may place an inmate in solitary confinement without requiring the director's permission (provided the inmate agrees). The statistics, however, only reflect the solitary confinements ordered by the director. If this is the case, the figures can only have a meaning for someone who is very familiar with the sector and knows what institutions have such decentralization. The figures are meaningless without this knowledge.

Meaning 6

In RCs 'A' and 'B', inmates are sometimes placed in solitary confinement for less than 24 hours in the context of the cooling-off policy: fast-track punishment. The cooling-off period is not included in the statistics. RC 'C' has no cooling-off period. Here, too, the figures only have a meaning for someone very familiar with the sector and have no meaning without this knowledge.

Meaning 7

There is considerable difference between the remand centres' policies on soft and hard drugs. The possession or use of drugs is punished in RCs 'A' and 'C' with placement in solitary confinement. This leads to relatively many placements. These placements thus are not only related to acts of violence, but also to the drug policy. So the figures have a very limited meaning in forming a judgment about acts of violence and sanctions imposed for them.

Meaning 8

There is a national placement commission, which is constantly faced with refusals by RCs 'B' and 'C' to admit inmates. Furthermore, as soon as inmates commit any violence, 'B' and 'C' will propose their transfer to another RC. RC 'A' rather has the attitude of solving its own problems (and so does not propose inmates for transfer) and accepting the inmates it is sent. The logical consequence of this attitude is a low number of acts of violence and sanctions at 'B' and 'C'.

This meaning may lead to the conclusion that 'B' and 'C' achieve poor performance, although performing well at first sight. This meaning can only be construed by someone with a lot of 'soft' knowledge of the sector.

Meaning 1 is poor and forces itself upon the person who only has the above figures available. Meanings 2 and 3 can still be construed by someone who has these figures, but can combine them with other, publicly available details. Meanings 4 to 8 are the most valuable and can only be construed by someone who has knowledge of the sector.

Anyone who construes a meaning based only on the figures resulting from the performance measurement may be virtually certain that this meaning will be poor or even incorrect. Most meanings resulting from a combination of the production figures with publicly available details (meanings 2 and 3) will also suffer this fate.

This makes the figures devoid of any meaning; at most, they may be a 'trigger' for obtaining a more accurate picture of acts of violence. Because several, partly competing, interpretations are possible, it is important that meaning giving is not monopolized. Monopolization means (1) that one actor decides (2) what figures are meaningful and (3) what meaning must be attached to these figures.

Lack of room to create a variety of meanings will not only lead to poor meaning giving, but reveal two other remarkable mechanisms.

- *The first meaning institutionalizes.* Meaning giving has an important temporal component. Lakoff points out that the first meaning that is formed tends to get lodged for a longer period. It becomes 'common sense'; change or replacement of this meaning is far from easy.[3] This may be very harmful. This applies to professionals when a meaning lodges itself among directors that does no justice to the multiplicity of a performance and is nevertheless guiding for policy development. It applies to directors when a meaning gets lodged that veils professional non-performance. The prohibition against monopolization does justice to the complexity of the profession, but as such it is also attractive to directors.
- *A focus on the 'outlier'.* This risk means that attention is paid only to performance that differs from the norm, from the historical trend or from the performance of other organizations.[4] Performance that does not differ does not trigger meaning giving. This may carry a risk, because the same performance may cover different realities. A richer picture is formed when different actors in an organization decide what performance qualifies for what meaning giving.

The prohibition against monopolization of meaning giving means that directors should allow professionals to give a meaning to the figures. In the above example, the prohibition against a monopoly on meaning giving also means that the various professionals (remand centre governors) are allowed to give their meaning to the figures. Of course, the director himself can also give his interpretation of the figures, which may give rise to a variety of meanings.

The opposite of monopolization, therefore, is variety: allowing more meanings will enable different meanings to compete and may prevent one (first) meaning from institutionalizing or attention being paid to 'outliers' only.[5] This necessary variety can be guaranteed by making agreements about what actors will be involved in the meaning giving of what figures (incidentally, a selection of figures that qualify for meaning giving will often be necessary, for reasons of efficiency, for example. Here, too, there is no comprehensiveness).

The prohibition against monopoly does not mean that no unambiguous meaning can evolve, but that it will result from a process in which different meanings compete. The prohibition against monopoly creates variety, from which a selection is then made. It thus offers a number of advantages:

- The meaning will be richer when there is a monopoly on meaning giving. If one meaning is the final result, then it will naturally be more authoritative.
- It the actors fail to arrive at one meaning, and if these meanings mutually conflict, then that is also an important fact. It may lead to reserve in the formulation of policy that conflicts with one of the meanings and that might have irreversible consequences.

The opportunity for both directors and professionals to give their meaning to the figures offers them scope (since establishing product figures and meaning giving are two different activities), which may be a disincentive for perverting behaviour.

3 Tolerance of a variety of product definitions and performance indicators; no comprehensive performance measurement

The literature makes frequent recommendations based on the idea that performance measurement should be a comprehensive system.

- 'The product budget defines *all* [italics by HdB] activities of the municipalities in terms of products (output) or effects (outcome) (. . .). The product budget is fully consistent with other policy and management tools.'[6]
- 'The goals [of the product budget, HdB] should be formulated clearly, unambiguously and measurably.'[7]

Concepts like 'comprehensive', 'consistent', 'clear' and 'unambiguous' are the ideograms of performance measurement (see Chapter 4): they reduce the complex reality so drastically that perverse effects are produced, but they are powerful, thus justifying all sorts of negative effects of comprehensiveness. The opposite view is that performance measurement is only one of the steering mechanisms in an organization. The underlying idea is simple: when a performance is multiple, measurement of this performance should also be multiple. Consequently, an organization should always have a certain variety of steering mechanisms.

Variety of systems: other systems of appraisal in addition to appraisal based on production

First, by using other systems of appraisal *in addition to* a system of output measurement.

- If performance measurement is used to allocate money, variety means that a certain percentage of the funds is allocated by means of performance measurement, whilst there are also other forms of allocation (lump sum, input, etc.), to which other appraisal mechanisms apply.
- If performance measurement is used to set a benchmark, output but also throughput might be compared: what are the work processes in an organization?

For professionals, such variety means that their performance is never appraised by means of performance measurement only. For a director, this means that in his policy making he is never fully dependent on the results of performance measurement. Such variety prevents unilateral appraisal, allows scope to both director and professionals (which moderates perversion) and also does justice to the complexity and multiplicity of public products.

Tolerate variety in the system of performance measurement

Second, by tolerating a variety of product definitions and performance indicators in the system. When the products of a professional organization are multiple, the same product can be defined and measured in several ways. A system of performance measurement that offers no room for it stands a fair chance of perverting.

I mentioned the example of the definition of a scientific publication earlier. In the world of the university it is customary to distinguish between scientific publications (meant for and reviewed by colleagues) and specialist publications (meant for a wider audience). The boundaries between these two types of publication may be vague, whilst great variety may exist within the two categories. This may prompt the question as to when an article deserves the predicate 'scientific'.

A scientist will nearly always have to account for his performance to different forums: within his own university, in a Dutch external review and against an international benchmark. If the same definition is used in different forums, given the variety of possible product definitions, the consequences are easy to predict. Substantial criticism is levelled against performance measurement because it is perceived as unfair and therefore creates perverse effects (since there is no room at all). This may affect the authority of performance measurement among professionals, which may cause it to become a mere book-keeping mechanism or a ritual.

Room is created if different forums tolerate different definitions. A scientist who, for example, receives no reward in forum X for a reviewed Dutch-language publication, may find appreciation for it in forum Y. This gives him scope, which does justice to the fact that an unambiguous definition of the product is impossible. It also adds to the fairness of the total appraisal.

If different product definitions are then found to lead to different appraisals of the scientific production (for example: 'moderate' at X and 'good' at Y), a management may regard this as a reason to differentiate its appraisals, for example by making agreements about the relation between Dutch-language and English-language publications in the future. If different product definitions receive the same appraisal ('moderate' at both X and Y), it will be more authoritative: whatever definition is chosen, the performance is substandard. This also makes a variety of product definitions attractive for directors. Tough appraisals are more authoritative, while they also show where qualification is necessary. An added advantage for directors is that it enables them to play the game of allowing scope on the one hand and managing on the other hand a little better. In X (in the example: intra-university performance measurement) he may opt for un-ambiguous product definitions and ambitious performance indicators, whereas in Y (for example: the international benchmark) there is far more room for product definitions and performance indicators chosen by the professional himself and for the new developments in the discipline.

In comprehensiveness thinking it is readily assumed that the same product definitions must be used in different forums. Those who accept, however, that professional activities are always multiple, will reach a different conclusion. If there are multiple products, different product definitions should be used.

To put it strongly, there are two opposite models. The model of comprehensiveness and consistency: steering focuses on all the products of an organization, everything an organization does is defined as a product and product definitions are unambiguous.

There is also a model of variety or even redundance: there are different systems to measure performance, different product definitions are used in these different systems and none of these systems claims to give a full picture of reality; different product definitions may even overlap.

Variety and redundance have a number of advantages.

- They moderate incentives for perverting behaviour, since professionals always have room: product definitions are not fixed or output does not determine the whole of the budget.
- The room offered by the system is also attractive for a director: he is less of a prisoner to the system and has room to set his own priorities, for example.
- Tolerance of variety can also be efficient. It relieves organizations of the burden of integrating all the different product definitions and attune them to each other.
- A redundant system produces authoritative outcomes, since one measurement system, without tolerance of variety, means that a simple picture is given of a multiple reality. If a redundant measurement system continues to present the same pictures (for example: performance as regards X and Y is substandard), it will be harder for the professional to ignore. Different channels keep sending the same signals, nevertheless doing justice to the multiplicity of the professional product. A redundant system will thus be more powerful than an integrated system. If different channels produce different pictures, this is also a given. Evidently, a positive or a negative appraisal may be given about a professional's production, which is highly dependent on the product definition chosen.
- Variety offers the possibility of dealing with the ambiguous picture of performance measurement. In system X, single product definitions and ambitious performance indicators can be chosen. The possibly perverse effects that may result from it may be moderated by offering room for innovation in other systems, for example, or by tolerating other product definitions.

Limits to variety

Figure 6.1 below shows that there are limits to this variety of product definitions and performance indicators. The tolerance of variety

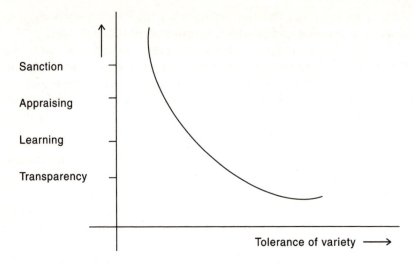

Figure 6.1 Relation between envisaged steering effect and tolerance of variety.

decreases in proportion as the envisaged steering effect of performance measurement increases. When the aim of a system is to learn, it may be useful to define the same product in a number of ways.

If a system is meant to allocate money, however, the tolerance of variety will be much lower. The use of different product definitions or performance indicators would seriously disturb the allocation process. In such a situation, variety may be reached by allowing alternative product definitions in the other systems of appraisal. Variety of or within systems thus creates communicating vessels:

- If tolerance of a variety of product definitions in a system of performance measurement is low, alternative product definitions or performance indicators in other systems of appraisal may be included.
- If tolerance of this variety in a system of performance measurement is high, fewer alternative systems of performance measurement will be necessary.

4 Types of products: differentiation and focus

If performance measurement can never be a comprehensive and consistent system, the obvious consequence is that an organization's products should be differentiated and the products on which an organization will focus should then be selected.

This differentiation may be based on two criteria: the relevance of the product and the nature of the product.

As regards the *relevance* of a product, it is customary to distinguish between the 'going concern' and the critical products in an organization. Products are critical when they are of strategic importance for an organization or when they involve risks for an organization. 'Going concern' involves products that are more operational and are, as a rule, made without too many problems.

As regards the *nature* of products a distinction may be made from the perspective of performance measurement between:

- single value products: products that are easy to define, while the product definition will change little as a rule;
- multi value products: products whose definition is an approach, which will consequently change frequently.

Figure 6.2 puts the two types of products together.

Professional organizations mainly generate multi value products, but always have unambiguous, single value products as well. A firm of organization consultants is largely professional. Its organizational advice is a multi value product. The consultancy also has a number of hard and easily measurable products: the length of time between the request for advice to the actual advice, for example. Education is a professional activity, but the time needed to mark exams is easy to measure and thus a single value product.

One of the lessons of performance measurement is that the search for completeness (all performance is included in the system) is not cost effective and creates an overload of information, which subsequently remains unused.[8] When an organization recognizes the differences between its products, a number of strategies are possible that will make it focus on a limited number of products.

It is remarkable that this does not happen very often. Research by Bordewijk and Klaassen in nine large Dutch municipalities shows that only two of these municipalities are able to resist the urge to

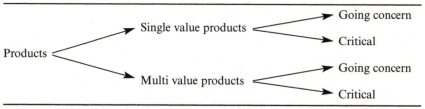

Figure 6.2 Differentiation in performance measurement.

extend and perfect the system of performance measurement. These two municipalities distinguish between types of tasks and say that performance measurement can only be applied to easily definable tasks.[9]

Focus on critical products

When the 'going concern' is running smoothly, a kind of 80/20 rule says that management and professionals can focus most of their attention on the critical products. In fact, the question as to what the critical products are can be answered interactively again. Management may invite the professionals to indicate what they feel are the critical products, and what performance is desirable or possible here.

Focus on single products

For professionals, many unambiguous products form the less interesting part of the work and may thus become the victims in the organization. This might be one of the first reasons why performance measurement might focus on this type of product. As regards multiple products, the professional ethos still guarantees quality, unlike single products. Performance measurement with a focus on single products thus has three advantages: it respects professional autonomy as regards critical products, focuses on products that receive little professional attention and also lend themselves to performance measurement. This prevents the watering-down of performance measurement, which is appropriate for multiple products, also affecting the unambiguous products.

Focus on single products; indirect steering of multiple products

It is equally important that a focus on an organization's single products may have positive side effects on its multiple products. The idea then is that proper and disciplined generation of single products imposes discipline on the generation of multiple products.

At an educational institution, performance in the services rendered to students can be measured, for example the number of exams marked within the agreed period, the making available of course material at least an 'x' number of weeks before the start of a course, etc. Steering focusing on these points imposes discipline in the generation of unambiguous products. Such discipline may then have its effects on multiple products: a self-evident attention for the questions and the world of students, a 'my word is my bond' culture, and so on. The steering effect of performance measurement on the multiple products is therefore given shape indirectly, through the unambiguous products.

Focus on going concern

Finally, an organization may choose to use performance measurement primarily for the going concern. The argument is that the critical products are so valuable for the organization, that they are the subject of discussion between management and professionals – beyond the scope of performance measurement – and are also subjected to the discipline of performance measurement to a lesser degree.

If management and professionals wish to form rich pictures of the critical products, if they want to prevent perverse effects or simply do not want to make agreements about production yet, it may be attractive to exclude them from performance measurement. This will change only when a crystallized picture of these products exits and, in a sense, they begin to form part of the 'going concern'.

7   Dynamic

Towards lively performance measurement

1 Introduction

Those who tolerate variety performance give measurement more content, since the same performance can be viewed from several perspectives and so have more than one meaning. Nevertheless, performance measurement thus still stays within the paradigm of product measurement. Performance measurement does not become really lively until products and the process of generation of these products are linked (see Table 4.2). This will be discussed in this chapter as follows.

*   Attention will be paid first to the need to consider both products and processes in appraising the performance of an authority and link them intelligently (Section 2). If an organization succeeds in doing so, this will improve the liveliness and the dynamic of performance measurement.
*   The question will then present itself how the game of performance measurement can be played, when both products and processes are appraised (Section 3).
*   In Section 4, I shall discuss the question how an organization should deal with new products and product definitions that evolve as a result of the dynamic inside and outside the organization (Section 4).

Performance measurement has so far been defined as the measuring of products. In this chapter, I shall add a dimension in Sections 2 and 3: performance measurement is the measuring of products, but also of processes.

2 The need for a hybrid system: product and process only have a meaning in relation to each other

Performance measurement becomes lively when it focuses not only on products, but also on processes. From a professional perspective, a strong accent is likely to be placed on processes. From a management and accountability perspective, the accent will rather be on products. Both perspectives are legitimate (Chapter 1).

This implies that the point is not the choice of either process or product, or that either of the two approaches should be superior. The point is that both approaches should be used simultaneously and that the conflict that exists between the two approaches should be utilized. Robert Quinn once referred to this as the 'management of competing values'.[1] I shall first give an example of this and then discuss this idea in more detail.

Example: community policing

The idea that a number of police officers are jointly responsible for the safety and liveability of a neighbourhood is gaining ground in many police forces. This phenomenon is known in the United States as 'community policing', in the Netherlands it is referred to as neighbourhood management.[2] A police commander must at some stage form a picture of the performance of the neighbourhood manager. This is difficult for an organization that heavily leans on product measurement. This is because the activities of a neighbourhood manager tend to be highly relational and also prevention-oriented. The neighbourhood manager makes particular agreements with residents and companies. He maintains his networks in the neighbourhood. He concludes that particular spots are unsafe and tries to improve their safety in consultation with the municipality. He organizes information campaigns, makes agreements with schools about timetables, with shopkeeper associations about joint checks, etc. The neighbourhood manager also has to perform the classic police tasks.

The neighbourhood manager's activities do not lend themselves to product measurement. The reason is that the link between his efforts and their results cannot be established unambiguously and his performance strongly depends on the efforts made by third parties (residents, shopkeepers). Product measurements have a limited meaning as regards activities of this kind and tend to create perverse effects if they are nevertheless used.

Instead, a form of process measurement would be more appropriate: the neighbourhood manager shows what activities he performs. Such process measurement can be conducted in all sorts of ways. The simplest and most informal form is a tour of the neighbourhood: the manager can show where his fixed contacts are, what changes have been made to buildings or in traffic, how particular neighbourhoods have been made safer and what shopkeepers are his fixed contacts. If youngsters cause the neighbourhood a lot of nuisance, the neighbourhood manager can demonstrate that he spends a great deal of time and effort on good relations with the parents of these youngsters. This process measurement thus gives meaning to production targets. If there is a lot of nuisance, but few official reports are made, this production figure is given meaning by the manager's information that he maintains lots of relations with parents.

Such process measurement may then be formalized, for example by adding up checklists. These may be adjusted on the basis of learning experiences ('living checklists'). As long as the appraiser is an internal reviewer (say, a commander) who is close to the professional process, he will often be able to form a good picture of the neighbourhood manager's performance. This is because he is a fellow-professional, who usually has sufficient expertise to distinguish good police work from bad policework.

All this does not mean, however, that there is no longer any room for product measurement in the appraisal. Both output and outcome figures may have an important function in the appraisal of the neighbourhood manager:

- *Output.* One output indicator is the number of official police reports about various types of offences. Given the neighbourhood's profile, the commander can form a picture of the number of official reports that can be made in the neighbourhood for particular offences. A production that remains far below the expected level may be a reason to ask the neighbourhood manager some critical questions about his process.
- *Outcome.* The number of reported thefts in a shopping centre shows a steady rise, the number of arrests remains the same. This would seem to be inconsistent with the efforts presented by the neighbourhood managers.

These production targets thus give rise to a new discussion with the neighbourhood manager. In some cases, the figures will *confirm* the pictures presented by process measurement. In other cases, the figures will *unmask* the pictures painted: crime is on the increase in the shopping centre and hardly any police reports are drawn up. Evidently, the police fail in visible presence. In some cases, these product figures will *qualify* the appraisal: a poorly organized process may nevertheless result in a good product (the reverse may be true as well).

Essence of the example: the movement between product and process

What is the essence of performance measurement as worked out in this example? The answer is simple: in his performance measurement, the commander constantly moves to and fro between process and product measurement. He uses product measurement to get a clearer picture of the process; process measurement also gives a meaning to production figures. Such a course of action has a number of advantages.

Product measurement: beyond the output–outcome debate

In the first place, the commander does not exclusively depend on product measurement, with all the bias inherent to it. When an organization exclusively relies on a system of product measurement and the perverse effects of it become manifest in course of time, all it can do is seek a solution within this system. As a result, systems of product measurement will continue to grow ('mushrooming') and problems within the system are solved by repairs to the system (additional product definitions and performance indicators). These repairs, however, will in turn create their perverse effects. The result is that the system will get out of control: it becomes so complex, that it may lose its steering effect (see Figure 7.1).

A number of problems cannot be solved within the system, however. The best-known example is the problem of the relation between output (for example: number of official police reports) and outcome (safe streets). The outcome not only depends on the performance of the relevant public organization, but also on that of other actors. Anyone who tries to include outcome in a system of performance measurement is bound to get stuck.

- Practically every linkage between output and outcome is disputable. If a professional is nevertheless held responsible for outcome, he is responsible for something he can influence only partially. This will be perceived as very unfair.
- If output and outcome are decoupled, however, there is a risk that a professional will simply produce, without paying any attention to the meaning of this production for the outcome.

A solution for these problems will always be unsatisfactory as long as it is sought only within the system of product measurement. This is completely different when process measurement is also given a place. The problematic relation between output and outcome should be no

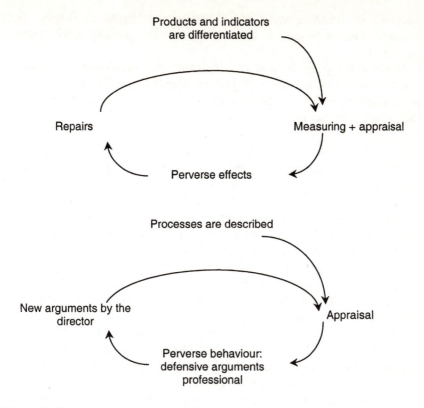

Figure 7.1 Consequences of a one-sided product or process approach.

reason to extend product measurement, but to use process measurement. Figures about output and outcome are not used to try to relate the two, but to ask the professional critical questions about his process. This leads to three conclusions. Output and outcome figures primarily trigger the forming of a picture about performance. These figures do not have any meaning until they are linked to process measurement. Relating product to process prevents the need for constant improvements and refinements in product measurement.

Process measurement: beyond the defensive dialogue

Secondly, process measurement creates its own perverse effects. A professional defends his own performance by building up a defensive line of reasoning. Figure 7.1 shows that this may also lead to the system of performance measurement getting out of control. The director may attempt to unmask these fallacies, but will, if he succeeds in doing so at all, call down new defensive reasoning upon himself. This may lead to an endless debate, without authoritative outcome.

When product measurement is used in addition to process measurement, a different picture will present itself. Defensive arguments by professionals, which might be mere fallacies, may be confronted with the production achieved by these professionals.

- In Chapter 4, I mentioned the example of a university offering highly fragmented study material. A first appraisal of it is likely to be negative: messy readers, containing a lot of overlap in the texts, are not conducive to the learning process and student results. Process measurement may present a totally different picture. The 'messy' study material is not a problem, but a solution for the new learning style of new generations of students: the 'homo zappiens'. Product measurement can never present this picture. Product measurement can, however, help to give a meaning to this picture. Suppose product measurement shows that students are making very little progress in their studies and that pass rates are very low. This may be a reason to ask the professionals critical questions about their views on learning styles. When product measurement then shows that teachers spend many hours on research and few hours on teaching, the use of the two performance measurement systems will have led to the following dynamic:
- The first conclusion was: messy and fragmented study material. This picture turned by 180 degrees in the discussion with the teachers (process measurement): today's student is a 'homo zappiens'; fragmented study material matches it. It is carefully compiled study material, based on a well-considered educational philosophy.
- Then there is product measurement: low pass rates, students stay at the university too long; there are few teacher hours available for education.
- The picture again turns by 180 degrees: not a well-considered educational philosophy, but 'homo zappiens' as an excuse for careless and sloppy education.
- This dynamic between the two performance measurement systems may then continue and may eventually present a differentiated picture: particular teachers have developed the educational philosophy sincerely and score good results; other teachers use this educational philosophy to justify sloppy conduct. Appraisal of these two types of teachers is clear. Other teachers have developed

their study material sincerely, but fail to score good results. It might be better not to appraise these teachers, and management and professionals will have to examine how they can learn more about the teaching and the study performance of 'homo zappiens' students.

This also leads to three conclusions. Process measurement may lead to the production of fallacies, which may partly be unmasked with the help of the results of product measurement. Process measurement is given a meaning by linking it to product measurement. Relating product to process prevents process measurement degenerating into an endless debate between directors and professionals.

Room for the game

The use of the two approaches allows the commander to play the performance measurement game. The neighbourhood manager presents a picture of the process, about which the commander can ask critical questions using product measurement. The neighbourhood manager is also able to play the game better. When product measurement leads to bad appraisal, he can demonstrate by means of process measurement that the maximum effort was made to prevent these figures. The use of the two approaches gives both of them *room* to play the game and so they are not dependent on one approach.

Once again: the boundary spanner

An organization that wants to use the two approaches and confront them critically with each other needs to identify the players that are able to do so. As in Chapter 6, the question at issue here is where in the organization is the 'boundary spanner' between the managerial system (where the product approach is likely to dominate) and the professional system (where a process approach is likely to dominate). The functioning of a performance measurement system will depend strongly on this boundary spanner. Without this boundary spanner, there is a risk that product orientation will force out process orientation or the reverse (Figure 7.2).

The boundary spanner should on the one hand be sufficiently close to the primary process to be able to use process measurement. On the other hand, the boundary spanner should also be sufficiently removed from the primary process to take a critical look at it and not fall victim to, for example, the non-intervention principle. On the one hand, the boundary spanner finds himself within the managerial

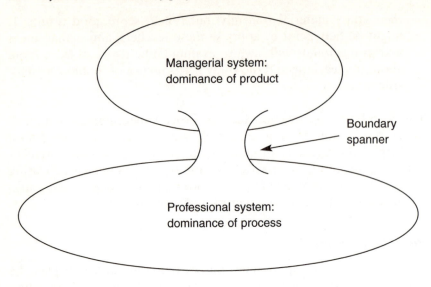

Figure 7.2 Product and process: the role of the boundary spanner

system to help account for an organization's performance. On the other hand, he is sufficiently removed from the managerial system, allowing him to put the meaning of product measurement into perspective.

3 A playing field between product and process indicators

A management that uses both product measurement and process measurement does justice to the complexity of professional activity. This enables performance measurement to become a lively activity.

Assumptions of performance measurement

The argument in the preceding section is based on two important assumptions.

- *The professional is cooperative*. The first assumption is that the professional will cooperate when performance measurement is lively. He is challenged by the game of product and process measurement and is prepared to participate in this game. Of course, this is not always so. For a professional who wants to cover up poor performance there are strong incentives not to participate in this game of product and process measurement. This will land the director in a difficult situation. A professor who publishes little (product) may raise the defence that he is conducting innovating and fundamental research and therefore cannot, or cannot yet, find time to publish (process). The court that passes few judgments (product) may defend itself by saying that it spends a lot of time on careful trade-offs of interests and will not allow itself to be rushed by figures about desirable output (process). Both may be right, but in both cases fallacies may be used to conceal poor performance. The game of product and process measurement may reveal a picture of this, but if there is no incentive for professionals to participate in this game, the only result will be a deadlock. Incidentally, the opposite picture may also present itself: the professor and the court that achieve high production, who take no interest in process measurement, because it might reveal that part of their production results from the perverting behaviour from Chapter 2.

• *Performance measurement is independent of the decision-making games in an organization.* A second assumption in the argument in Section 2 is that performance measurement is an autonomous activity, completely detached from the other subjects at issue between director and professional. This assumption, too, is not automatically correct. Many professional organizations have the characteristics of a network organization.[3] Interdependencies exist between the various players in the organization (management, various professionals), causing most of the decisions in such organizations to be reached through consultation and negotiation. Decision making is a constant process of linking the problems of the one party to the solutions of the other party. A professional who is not prepared to provide accountability can use his interdependent relationship with a director: a lenient appraisal of his performance by the director is then exchanged for the professional's support for a director's goals as regards another subject. Such linkage between performance measurement and other subjects is likely to be sophisticated. The game of product and process measurement is played, but it is not aimed at forming a rich picture. It degenerates into a game of give and take.

Risks

From the perspective of the director, these assumptions pose two risks. The first risk is that a conflict will erupt between professional and director about the performance achieved, in which the one party relies on product measurement and the other party relies on process measurement. The literature about network organizations always warns against conflicts of this type. A conflict between parties that are mutually dependent, which is confined to one spectrum (in this case: product versus process), never produces any winners. Even if one of the parties bulldozes its own view through, this may harm future relations with the loser to such an extent as to turn the winner into a loser as well. This prompts the question as to how to prevent the game between director and professional being one-dimensional.[4]

The second risk is that the director frantically attempts to make performance measurement an autonomous activity and thus single it out from an important institution in network organizations: decision making is give and take. The network literature also warns against this. Conditional reasoning would be more sensible than to resist institutions: decision making is a matter of give and take; consequently, so is performance measurement. A director should not prevent this, but make use of it: how can the game of give and take be used in order to achieve the goals of performance measurement?[5]

The need for a multidimensional playing field

The first response to this question is that it is important to create a multidimensional playing field. This is possible, for example, by not only using the product–process dimension, but also the ex post/sanction–ex ante/learn dimension. Figure 7.3 shows that this creates a playing field.

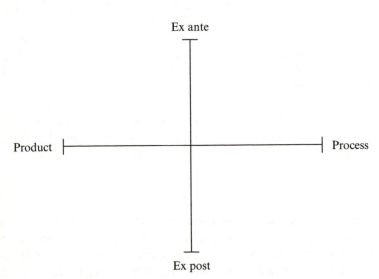

Ex ante

Product   Process

Ex post

Figure 7.3 A playing field for performance measurement.

Such a playing field creates room for both the director and the professional to manoeuvre and so prevent deadlocks. The risk of deadlocks increases when movement is only possible in the product–process dimension.

- Such a deadlock will – for example – occur when a director concludes that production by a professional unit is low, while the unit in question relies on process-type arguments (a lot of innovation, so no production; carefulness comes before production; see the examples of the professor and the court).
- Both the director and the professional may extend their lines of reasoning without a common view being created. The director concludes that other professional units also innovate, without their production falling behind. The professional objects that his process differs from that of other units on a number of points, which bars comparison. New arguments will be used in the next round, without leading to a fruitful discussion.
- This discussion will focus mainly on the past, which will only worsen the deadlock. This is because the past is fixed: the production has been achieved, the process has been designed.
- At some stage, a director who feels that part of these arguments are mere fallacies would be wise to leave the discussion about the past for what it is and invite the professional to make agreements about the future. A reactive discussion about past performance may then be turned into a proactive discussion about future performance. The professor with his innovative research may be invited to indicate when production will be forthcoming. If none can be expected, interim reports may be impossible, which, for example, might be discussed with a fellow professional. Because the discussion moves on the ex ante–ex post axis, movement is also possible on the product–process axis. The director who concludes that other professionals also innovate, without their production lagging behind, may attempt to convert this conclusion into agreements about the future rather than carry on a discussion about the past.
- This may lead to the professional's commitment to improvement of production or, if such improvement is actually impossible, better appraisal of the process. This commitment will facilitate appraisal in the next round. It is worth noting, however, that a director who wants to urge a professional to adopt a more proactive attitude, may, prior to this, have to discuss the past. This is because agreements about the future have more value when it is clear to the parties that they partly spring from displeasure with

past performance. It would, of course, be very helpful for the negotiating position of a poorly performing professional to centre the discussion on the future straightaway.

The advantage of a playing field is that it offers room to the players (management and professionals) and the debate may be based on product measurement, but also on process measurement. Appraisal of the past is possible, but so are agreements about the future. Room means that parties can manoeuvre in the performance measurement game.

Performance measurement as a game of give and take

The above does not mean that the professional will automatically feel committed to performance to be achieved in the future. This takes me to the second answer to the question of how the network structure of professional organizations can be dealt with.

Decision making in network organizations is a game of give and take. The various players in the network organization constantly play a game in which the problems of the one player are linked to the solutions of the other player. It is impossible for a director to avoid this, but it is possible to make use of it.

The director may link the agreements about future performance that he makes with the professional to other subjects. This may create a form of reward for the professional if he complies with the agreements. Performance may result in a higher allocation of funds, extra facilities or a more important role for the professional in establishing the strategy of the organization. Of course, negative sanctions are also possible in the event of non-performance, or performance may prevent particular negative sanctions (no cuts in the budget if the performance is achieved, no cuts in facilities, no exclusion from strategy making).

To link agreements about performance to other subjects may be an extra incentive for the professional to actually live up to the agreements. After all, agreements about the future can also be used to prevent appraisal of the past.

The essence here is that a playing field should be created that comprises more than one dimension and where more issues are at stake than mere performance measurement. This creates room. The director may subsequently sanction meeting the performance promised by linking it to other subjects.

A warning should be given here, however, that a director can, of course, never completely control this game. The game is played in interaction with the professional, who will also attempt to use his influence in the appraisal of the past and in making agreements about the future. Furthermore, this game can only be effective if the professional is capable of improvement. If a professional performs badly and if he has reached the ceiling of his possibilities, performance measurement can only have a meaning in making this transparent.

4 The dynamic of performance measurement

Every system of product definitions presents a temporary picture of the products of the organization. Products of organizations develop as a result of both *internal* and *external* dynamic. If performance measurement is to be lively, then the system of performance measurement will have to adapt itself to this dynamic.

Internal and external dynamic

Every system of performance measurement has a limited life: performance measurement will cease to be effective after some time.[6] The explanation may be a negative one: given a system of performance measurement, the professional learns how to optimize his behaviour, which will cause the system to pervert (see Chapters 2 and 3). The design principles discussed in Part Two of this book can make performance measurement more trustful, meaningful and lively, but at some stage the system of performance measurement will have lost its effect. The explanation may also be positive: performance measurement has had sufficient beneficial effect at some stage and is no longer useful.

Suppose the management of an educational institution is dissatisfied with the long time it takes students to complete their studies. On average, it takes students over six years to complete a four-year study programme. They suffer delay particularly during their graduation phase because they are not given proper counselling. In reaction to this, the management decides to tie future funding to the number of master's degrees awarded. Every master's degree generates an amount of money, the rule being that this amount decreases in proportion as studies last longer. This performance indicator will lose its effect after a number of years. The number of master's degrees will first rise and then stabilize (evidently no further improvement is possible). The performance indicator was an incentive for performance but degenerates into a bookkeeping mechanism for settling accounts. Such is the life of every performance indicator; it calls for other indicators.

This is the internal dynamic of performance measurement. There is also external dynamic: the environment in which an organization works will change and demand new or different performance measurement.

For example, a ministry has an implementing organization that draws the attention of companies to the possibility of applying for subsidies in particular fields of technology. Advisers employed by this implementing organization visit companies for this purpose. The implementing organization annually provides a number of production figures to the ministry, including a figure indicating the number of applications for subsidies in relation to the number of company visits. Over the years, this figure shows a development in the wrong direction: there is a rapid increase in the number of company visits needed for one application. The explanation is that the environment of the implementing organization has changed; there are now other authorities that also offer subsidies in the field of technology in question. The advisers have adapted their strategy to this: within companies, they now identify projects that qualify for subsidies and subsequently examine what authorities can be asked to subsidize these projects. The guideline they follow is to see first what European funds are available, then what funds the other ministries make available and finally what funds lower authorities have available. Only when none of these authorities has an appropriate subsidy scheme do they examine what subsidies their own ministry can offer. The introduction of this strategy has raised the number of applications for subsidy per company visited, but caused a fall in the number of subsidy applications to the ministry concerned per company visited. The environment has changed, the enterprising professional has reacted adequately, but the system of performance measurement still measures the old performance.

Dynamic and the need for stability

In these and similar situations, performance measurement has a coagulating effect: it does not move with the dynamic of product development. One of the consequences may be that performance measurement slows down innovation or that, if innovation does take place, the professional feels that he has been sold short. He innovates, but cannot make it visible in the figures and is not evaluated by it. I distinguish three types of innovation here, summarized in Table 7.1.

Innovation always gives rise to a conflict, which has already been discussed in Chapter 4. On the one hand, a system should be adaptive: it should be capable of adjusting to changed circumstances. On the other hand, a system should be stable enough if it is to fulfil its

Table 7.1 First-, second- and third-order changes and matching rules of the game

Type of change	Rule of the game from the perspective of change	Rule of the game from the perspective of stability
First order: new performance within the existing system of products	Professional and director arrive at meaning giving by interacting	Not applicable
Second order: new products	Professional or director may identify new products	New product is included in the system if it is proved functional
Third order: new systems of performance measurement	Professional or director may indicate dysfunctions in the existing system and propose alternatives	New system always functions in addition to the existing system, relative meaning of the systems changes.

functions. Functions like comparing, appraising and sanctioning are more difficult to fulfil when a system keeps changing. Table 7.1 contains rules of the game for each type of change from the perspective of dynamic and from the perspective of stability.

First order: new performance

Once product definitions have been given, changes in production may occur; for example, more is produced of one product and less of another. In the jargon of corporate management: shifts occur in the portfolio.

It is particularly important here to prevent such a shift from being given a one-sided interpretation. The matching rule of the game therefore concerns the 'meaning making rights': when a shift occurs, both the professional and the director should be allowed to give a meaning to it. They can then, in a process of interaction, try to reach agreement about this meaning or a clear picture of their difference of opinion about it. See Chapter 6, Section 2, about the importance of meaning giving. First-order changes occur within the system of performance measurement. The conflict between change and stability therefore does not occur here.

Second order: new products

Second-order change means that new products are developed or that an organization (management or professional) feels a need to make existing products visible with the help of new definitions.

The matching rule of the game is that the management and the professional must be allowed to define new products and make them visible. This may be in the interest of either of them. That of the director, for example, because his environment demands a different type of accountability; that of the professional, because innovations in the primary process have given rise to new products.

The need for stability can be served by a rule of the game saying that new products will only be admitted to the system of performance measurement once they have proved to be functional. The director or professional who wants to introduce a new product is allowed room beyond the existing system of performance measurement:

- to define new products;
- to indicate what they mean for the existing product definitions;
- to define performance indicators for them;
- to provide production targets for the organization's new products;
- to indicate what influence these production targets will have on existing production.

Once these new products have proved their meaning, they may lead to a change in the portfolio and be given a place in the performance measurement system.

Such a rule of the game prevents all too easy criticism of the existing system. It forces management and professionals to give an accurate description of the new products. Once the functionality of the new product definition has been proved, it may be included in the existing system of performance measurement. This protects the integrity of the system: it is not burdened with product definitions that still have to prove their right of existence or of which it is unclear how they relate to existing products.

Third order: the system of performance measurement is adjusted

Finally, the conclusion may also be that performance measurement has a coagulating effect, not because of a shift in production or because new products have evolved, but because the system of performance measurement itself causes coagulation. Management or professionals may find that a number of years of performance measurement have affected the organization's innovative power and vitality. This is why it might be sensible to make room for ambitious plans again, changing over from output financing to input financing. Other tools can also play a role in revitalizing the profession: new types of benchmarks, forms of competition between professional units, new audits or even 'goal-free budgeting' (a professional is allocated funds without preconditions and accounts for them later).

Here, too, it is sensible to regularly discuss this existential question in the dialogue between management and professionals. The rule of the game from the perspective of adjustment is that both can put up the dysfunctions of performance measurement for discussion and put forward proposals for alternatives. Given the tendency of performance measurement to develop into a resistant system (Chapter 3), the rule of the game that the system itself may be the subject of debate in the dialogue between management and professional is of great importance.

What is the rule of the game from the perspective of stability? In Chapter 6, the design principle of 'variety' was discussed. One of the effects of this principle is that performance measurement always exists in addition to other systems of appraisal; performance measurement is a partial and not a comprehensive steering mechanism. The more comprehensive performance measurement (which implies: the less room for other steering mechanisms), the stronger the perverse effect.

If there are other mechanisms apart from performance measurement, a change of system will be less radical than expected: the relative position of performance measurement changes in favour of other systems of appraisal.

Suppose an organization has three systems of appraisal: part of the budget is divided through performance measurement, part of it on the basis of plans submitted (input) and part is divided on the basis of activities performed (throughput). Suppose it is subsequently found that performance measurement produces nothing but perverse effects now and is itself up for discussion. Abolition of performance measurement has two major disadvantages: input and throughput steering will also have their perverse effects after some time (see Chapter 1), while abolition may be a form of destruction of organizational capital (as a rule, an organization makes considerable investments in a system of performance measurement, Chapter 3). A change of system may also mean that the meaning of performance measurement is reduced when funds are allocated (see Table 7.2). This

Table 7.2 The relative meaning of a change of system

t_0	Performance			Input	Throughput
t_1	Performance	Input		Throughput	

has at least three advantages: (1) when the perverse effects of input and throughput steering become manifest, performance measurement may be reactivated; (2) capital destruction is prevented: the organization remains familiar with performance measurement; (3) incentives for perversion are less strong because performance measurement has a limited position.

From the perspective of dynamic, the rule of the game is slightly paradoxical. When management and professionals conclude that a system of performance measurement is no longer effective, the system is not abandoned, but its relative position changes. For example, it is given a peripheral position for the time being, but it can always return to a more central position. An important theme in this book is that a moderate use should be made of performance measurement. If not, perverse effects will dominate. Consequently, moderation also applies to the need to change the system: it would be wiser to change the relative position of a system of performance measurement (temporarily) than to abolish it.

Part III

8 The paradoxes of performance measurement

The first chapters of this book have presented an ambiguous picture of performance measurement. On the one hand, it has its beneficial effects; on the other hand, it invites perverse behaviour. What should the final appraisal of performance measurement be? I shall give my appraisal in the form of seven paradoxes in performance measurement.

I would point out first that the answer to the above question is always context-related, of course. An organization with a strong internal orientation may benefit greatly from performance measurement; this may be entirely different for an organization that has long been heavily oriented towards output. Furthermore, performance measurement moves through a kind of cycle. When a system of performance measurement is introduced, its beneficial effects will initially become clear, but the perverse effects will eventually dominate.

Paradox 1: the more steering pretensions, the less effective

Performance measurement used as a tool for hierarchical steering will harm its own effectiveness. The more functions a director wants to create with the help of performance measurement (transparency, learning, appraising, sanctioning, comparing), the more its effectiveness will decline. The more hierarchy and the more functions, the stronger the incentive to pervert a system. Furthermore, the risk of hierarchical use is that performance measurement will ritualize. Although performance indicators and production figures are provided, they have little to do with the actual course of business in an organization. If they do, a system of performance measurement may form a layer of rock between management and professionals. It deprives management of its insight into the professional process. This is the first paradox: the more steering pretensions performance measurement has to meet, the less effective it will be (Chapter 2, Chapter 6).

Paradox 2: good performance is punished

The more performance measurement develops as a management tool, the poorer its content; it degenerates into a form of bookkeeping. There is every risk that the system of performance measurement will pervert. Furthermore, when a system of performance measurement is poor, it is attractive for the poorly performing professional. It will always offer possibilities to somehow make poor performance look respectable. Closely related to this is another mechanism: performance measurement rewards good performance, but it only works when the differences between the organizations concerned are not too big. If they are, strong incentives may arise to impose extra targets on well-performing organizations and to spare a poorly performing organization. This is because this reaction is likely to cause less conflict than sanctioning poor performance. Furthermore, three types of arguments are available for such a reaction: (1) performance measurement does not register poor performance, but explains it (performance measurement makes the rich richer and the poor poorer); (2) many public products are indispensable and non-substitutable, so a moderate reaction to poor performance is necessary; (3) sanctions on poor performance are rarely an incentive for better performance. This may give rise to the situation where an organization is spared if it performs poorly and is not rewarded or even punished if it performs well. This is the second paradox: good performance may be punished by a system of performance measurement (Chapter 2, Chapter 6).

Paradox 3: orientation towards products and output will only have a meaning if orientation towards processes and throughput is developed as well

Throughput steering rewards activities (the number of beds occupied in a hospital) and is a disincentive for results. The opposite is steering that rewards output results (products).

Performance measurement will pervert if it focuses on products only (output). A one-sided orientation towards processes (throughput) also creates perverse effects. Performance measurement will therefore always have to focus on products as well as processes. Product measurement has no meaning until it is related to process measurement. The same applies to process measurement: a meaningful picture can only evolve in combination with product measurement.

This is the third paradox: product measurement (output) only becomes meaningful by relating it to the 'competing value' of process measurement (throughput). Output steering is often presented as an alternative for throughput steering, but actually the one cannot exist without the other.

This has its consequences for the possibilities of appraising an organization's performance on the basis of performance measurement. The results of performance measurement may be less unambiguous and multi-interpretable, which should lead to reserve in an appraisal. However, if product measurement and process measurement present the same picture, this may produce an even more authoritative appraisal than one based exclusively on product or process measurement (Chapter 1, Chapter 7).

Paradox 4: a system of performance measurement only works if the system offers room to moderate the system's consequences

Performance measurement will only be effective if it offers a director and professionals room. This room concerns, among other things, the question how products are defined, how production is appraised and how systems of central and decentralized performance measurement relate to each other. Room always means that the answers to these and similar questions result from interaction between management and professionals. Performance measurement tends to be introduced in the belief that it establishes clear and unambiguous standards for the appraisal of authorities. 'Performance management sends employees unmistakeble signals about which results matter, and it rewards them when they produce those results',[1] say the performance measurement gurus. Actually, a system of performance measurement only works if there is room for management and professionals to moderate the consequences of performance measurement, which requires all sorts of consultations. Room limits the incentives for perverting behaviour and does justice to the fact that performance measurement is a simple mechanism to appraise multiple performance (Chapter 2, Chapters 5 and 6).

Paradox 5: orientation towards products reduces the interaction costs of the director, but brings on interaction costs for the 'boundary spanner' at the intermediate level of the organization

There is a sharp conflict between managerial rationality and professional rationality. Managerial rationality evokes an interest in information that makes it possible to account for performance and can play a role in managerial processes. Performance measurement will be evaluated by this standard. Professional rationality evokes an interest in information that presents a rich picture of the multiplicity of the profession.

Performance measurement is embedded in these two rationalities, which poses risks: one rationality may start to dominate the other. Consequently, proper functioning of performance measurement mainly depends on the boundary spanners between the managerial and the professional system. These are actors that are often found somewhere on the intermediate level of an organization and that function both in the managerial and in the professional system. It is important to identify these boundary spanners, and both management and professionals should allow them room to shape performance measurement so that it will be meaningful for the director as well as for the professionals.

There is a paradox here, too. One advantage of performance measurement – the theory teaches us – is that it minimizes interaction costs between the director and professionals. The director is only interested in output, not in the way a product is generated. The risk is that a gap may develop between the director and the professionals. This means an important role for the boundary spanner, whose interaction costs are necessarily high (Chapters 6 and 7).

Paradox 6: performance measurement will only be effective if it has a limited meaning for directors and professionals

A limited meaning implies that performance measurement has a limited number of functions and is used for a limited number of forums. It can never be a comprehensive appraisal system: it always functions along with other systems of appraisal. If these rules are ignored, director and professionals will become the prisoners of the system and very strong incentives for perverting behaviour will develop. Furthermore, if there is a comprehensive system, all problems within this system should be solved. This will increase the complexity of the system so much that it will lose its function. If a system is comprehensive, then an organization also loses its manoeuvrability and the change-over to other systems of appraisal will be very expensive.

Also, performance measurement will only function when there is a certain tolerance of variety and overlap. Given the multiple character of an authority's performance, a system that only comprises unambiguous product definitions will lack meaning. Products can be defined in several ways, product definitions may change, the same definition may cover several realities and performance can be interpreted in several ways. Relations between directors and professionals will have to offer scope for such a variety of product definitions and interpretations of performance (Chapters 5, 6 and 7).

Paradox 7: Performance measurement, too, is a game of consultation and negotiation

Systems of performance measurement are always embedded in the interdependent relationship between director and professional. Most of the contact between them will comprise negotiations; so a system will always have to offer scope for the game of consultation and negotiation. Performance measurement thus always requires a playing field that offers room for director and professionals and allows both to achieve their own values: accountability and respect for the profession. Here, too, a paradox appears: performance measurement is based on the idea that it enables sanctioning on the basis of performance. In a professional environment, however, sanctioning is the result of negotiation (Chapter 7).

All this leads to the final picture that performance measurement can be beneficial, but only if very moderate use is made of it. Once an organization has introduced a system of performance measurement, it will have to practise this moderation systematically, by allowing room for interaction, variety and dynamic. This is not easy, because performance measurement looks promising and there is every temptation to use it as a powerful steering instrument.

Notes

1 An introduction to performance measurement

1 For example P. van der Knaap, 'Resultaatgerichte verantwoordelijkheid', in *Bestuurskunde,* Elsevier, The Hague, 2000, no. 5, pp. 237–47.

2 David Osborne and Ted Gaebler, *Reinventing Government*, Penguin, Reading, Massachusetts, 1992; David Osborne and Peter Plastrik, *The Reinventor's Fieldbook. Tools for Transforming Your Government*, Jossey Bass, San Francisco, 2000; Geert Bouckaert and Tom Auwers, *Prestaties meten in de overheid*, Die Keure, Bruges, 1999; I also refer to three scientific journals with a great many articles about performance measurement: *Accounting, Auditing and Accountability Journal; Managerial Auditing Journal; Public Productivity and Management Review*. International comparisons: see the PUMA (Public Management) activities of the OECD (http://www.oecd.org/puma/) and Geert Boeckaert, Dieter Hoes and Wim Ulens, *Prestatiemeetsystemen in de overheid: een internationale vergelijking*, Die Keure, Bruges, 2000; Uit de hoek van accountancy: H. den Boer and L.C. van Zutphen, *Business Control and Auditing*, Schoonhoven; J.G.W. Broen, A.C. de Jong and A.A. Kooijmans, *Besturing en beheersing*, Kluwer, Deventer, 2002; H. Thomas Johnson, *Relevance Lost. The Rise and Fall of Managament Accounting*, Harvard Business School Press, Boston, 1991.

3 Particularly in many general management handbooks, for example in David Boddy and Robert Paton, *Management. An Introduction*, Prentice Hall, London, 1998, p. 65.

4 Robert D. Behn and Peter A. Kant, 'Strategies for avoiding the pitfalls of performance contracting', *Public Productivity and Management Review* (1999), vol. 22, no. 4, pp. 470–89, p. 477.

5 See for example G. Frerks, 'Performance measurement in foriegn policy: security policy, proper governance, conflict prevention and human rights', in *Towards result-oriented accountability*, Ministry of Foreign Affairs, The Hague, 2000, pp. 17–24 (in Dutch).

6 C.N Parkinson, *Parkinsons's Law,* Penguin, New York, 1964.

7 David Osborne and Ted Gaebler, *Reinventing Government*, Penguin, Reading, Massachusetts, 1992 pp. 147–50.

8 Jane S. Durch *et al., Improving Health in the Community*, National Academy Press, Washington D.C., 1997.

9 Also see Ted Gaebler *et al., Positive Outcomes. Raising the Bar on Government Reinvention*, Chatelaine Press, Burke, Virginia, 1999, p. 201.

10 David Osborne and Ted Gaebler, *Reinventing Government*, Penguin, Reading, Massachusetts, 1992, p. 146.

11 David Osborne and Ted Gaebler, *Reinventing Government*, Penguin, Reading, Massachusetts, 1992, pp. 138–9.

12 Delft University of Technology, *An Evaluation of the Use of the University Allocation Model 1996–1999*, Delft University of Technology (DUT), Delft, 2000 (in Dutch).

13 David Osborne and Peter Plastrik, *Banishing Bureaucracy*, Perseus Press, Reading, 1997, p. 145.

14 R.J. in 't Veld, *Relations Between the State and Higher Education*, Kluwer Law International, The Hague, 1996, pp. 79–80.

15 For the differences between so-called R-professionals and I-professionals (routine and innovative respectively), see M. Weggeman, *Leidinggeven aan professionals*, Samsom, Deventer, 1994, p. 29.

16 Hans Broere, *Symbol City*, Netherlands School of Public Administration (NSOB), The Hague, 2001, p. 28.

17 G. Frerks, 'Performance measurement in foreign policy: security policy, proper governance, conflict prevention and human rights', in *Towards Result-oriented Accountability*, Ministry of Foreign Affairs, The Hague 2000, pp. 21 (in Dutch); also A.G. Dijkstra, 'Performance measurement in foreign aid', in *Beleidsanalyse* (2000), pp. 13–19 (in Dutch).

18 P. van der Knaap and R. van den Broek, 'A result-oriented governance model for the judiciary', in *Bestuurskunde* (2000), pp. 313–25 (in Dutch).

19 See for example Ted Gaebler *et al.*, *Positive Outcomes. Raising The Bar On Government Reinvention*, Chatelaine Press, Burke, Virginia 1999, p. 198.

20 In fact, this applies to all literature about performance measurement, so not only to the literature relating to the public sector. Take for example the well-known Balanced Score Card. No matter how it may be considered, what is good about it is that it forces users to view corporate performance from several perspectives. See for example *Harvard Business Review on Measuring Corporate Performance*, Boston, 1998.

21 David Osborne and Peter Plastrik, *The Reinventor's Fieldbook. Tools for Transforming Your Government*, Jossey Bass, San Francisco, 2000, p. 225.

22 Geert Boeckaert and Ton Auwers, *Measuring Performance in Government*, Die Keure, Bruges, 1999, p. 38.

23 Geert Boeckaert and Ton Auwers, *Measuring Performance in Government*, Die Keure, Bruges, 1999, p. 80.

24 Geert Boeckaert and Ton Auwers, *Measuring Performance in Government*, Die Keure, Bruges, 1999, p. 38.

25 R. Klein and N. Carter, 'Performance measurement: a review of concepts and issues', in D. Beeton (ed.) *Performance Measurement. Getting the Concepts Right*, Public Finance Foundation, London, 1988.

26 See for example K.A. Van Peursem, M.J. Pratt and S.R. Lawrence, 'Health management performance. A review of measures and indicators', in *Accounting, Auditing and Accountability Journal* (1995), no. 5, pp. 34–70, p. 60.

2   The perverse effects of performance measurement

1 See David Osborne and Ted Gaebler, *Reinventing Government*, Penguin, Reading, Massachusetts, 1992, Appendix B; David Osborne and Peter Plastrik, *The Reinventor's Fieldbook. Tools for Transforming Your Government*, Jossey Bass, San Francisco, 2000.

2 Allard Hoogland, 'Het OM in de beklaagdenbank', *Hollands Maandblad* (1998) no. 2.

3 James Q. Wilson, *Bureaucracy: What Government Agencies Do and Why They Do It*, Basic Books, New York, 2000.

4 J.A. Winston, on www.city.grande-prairie.ab.ca/perfm_a.htm#Top

5 Robert D. Behn and Peter A. Kant, 'Strategies for avoiding the pitfalls of performance contracting', in *Public Productivity and Management Review* (1999), vol. 22, no. 4, pp. 470–89, p. 474; Smith, P. (1993), 'Outcome-related performance indicators and organizational control in the public sector', *British Journal of Management*, vol. 4, pp. 135–51, pp. 146–8.

6 This is an often heard objection to performance measurement within universities, see for example a debate in the *Academische Boekengids* (2000) and (2001), nos 23–6.

7 Nancy Zollers and A.K. Ramanathan, 'For-profit charter schools and students disabilities: the sordid side of the business of schooling', *Phi Delta Kappan* (December 1998), vol. 81, pp. 297ff; Thomas A. Good and Jennifer S. Braden, *The Great School Debate: Choice, Vouchers, and Charters*, Laurence Erlbaum Association Inc., New Jersey, 1999.

8 John F. Witte, *The Market Approach to Education: An Analysis of America's First Voucher Program*, Princeton University Press, Princeton 2000.

9 Jeroen Trommelen, 'Negentig procent moet dood', in *de Volkskrant*, 8 February 2001, p. 13.

10 H.G. Sol, 'Aggregating data for decision support', in *Decision Support Systems* (1985), vol. 1, no. 2, pp. 111–21.

11 Example found in a short article by John J. Videler, 'De domme willekeur van het beoordelingssysteem', in *Academische Boekengids* (2001), p. 16.

12 Mary Bowerman and Shirley Hawksworth, 'Local government internal auditors' perceptions of the Audit Commission', *Managerial Auditing Journal* (1999), vol. 14, no. 8, pp. 396–407.

13 This is not different in the private sector of course. As a product, a jar of peanut butter is a trade-off between, for example, economic, ecological and safety considerations.

14 Garry D. Carnegie and Peter W. Wolnizer, 'Enabling accountability in museums', *Accounting, Auditing and Accountability Journal* (1996), no. 5, pp. 84–99.

15 For this mechanism see for example Coen Teulings, *Privatisering in het tijdsgewricht van recollectivisering*, OCFEB, Rotterdam 2000; Smith calls this a 'Tunnel vision': concentration on aspects included in the performance management system, to the exclusion of other important areas. P. Smith (1993), 'Outcome-related performance indicators and organizational control in the public sector', *British Journal of Management*, vol. 4, pp. 135–51, pp. 141–2. See also M. Goddard, R. Mannion and P. Smith (2000), 'Enhancing performance in health care: a theoretical perpspective on agency and the role of information', *Economics of Health Care Systems*, vol. 9 issue 2, pp. 95–107.

16 Anthony L. Iaquito, 'Can winners be losers? The case of the Deming prize for quality and performance among large Japanese manufacturing firms', *Managerial Auditing Journal*, 1999, vol. 14, no. 1/2, pp. 28–35.

17 Information Hans Buddendijk; Court Manager, District Court Maastricht, The Netherlands.

18 Edward B. Fiske and Helen F. Ladd, *When Schools Compete. A Cautionary Tale*, The Brooking Institution, Washington, 2000.

19 From F.L. Leeuw, 'Performance auditing, new public management and performance improvement: questions and answers', *Accounting, Auditing and Accountability Journal* (1996) vol. 9, no. 2, pp. 92–102; F.L. Leeuw, 'Onbedoelde

neveneffecten van outputsturing, controle en toezicht?', *Raad voor Maatschappelijke Ontwikkeling*, *Aansprekend burgerschap*, RMO, The Hague 2000, pp. 149–71.

20 From F.L. Leeuw, 'Performance auditing, new public management and performance improvement: questions and answers', *Accounting, Auditing and Accountability Journal* (1996) vol. 9, no. 2, pp. 92–102; F.L. Leeuw, 'Onbedoelde neveneffecten van outputsturing, controle en toezicht?', *Raad voor Maatschappelijke Ontwikkeling*, *Aansprekend burgerschap*, RMO, The Hague 2000, pp. 149–71.

21 P. Bordewijk and H.L Klaasen, *Don't Think You Can Measure Us*, VNG uitgevers, The Hague, 2000, pp. 97–8.

22 See for example John A. Scott, *Seeing Like A State, How Certain Schemes to Improve the Human Condition Have Failed*, Yale University Press, New Haven, 1998, pp. 313–29.

23 John A. Scott, *Seeing Like A State, How Certain Schemes to Improve the Human Condition Have Failed*, Yale University Press, New Haven, 1998, pp. 313–29.

24 Distilled from Paul Martens, *Amerika-Amsterdam v.v.*, Netherlands School of Public Administration (NSOB), The Hague, 2001.

25 See David Osborne and Ted Gaebler, *Reinventing Government*, Penguin, Reading, Massachusetts, 1992; David Osborne and Peter Plastrik, *The Reinventor's Fieldbook. Tools for Transforming Your Government*, Penguin, San Francisco, 2000, p. 355.

3   The resistance of perverted performance measurement

1 R.J. in 't Veld has pointed this out in particular. Performance indicators have a limited life, are subject to the Law of Decreasing Effectiveness, as a result of which perverse effects will eventually become dominant. R.J. in 't Veld, *Relations between the State and Higher Education*, Kluwer Law International, The Hague, 1996, p. 36 and p. 79; R.J. in 't Veld, *The Dynamics of Educational Performance Indicators*, Ministry of Education, Culture and Science (OC&W), The Hague, 1987.

2 M. Hoogwout, 'Comptabiliteitsvoorschriften op de schop', *Overheidsmanagement* (2000), no. 4, pp. 94–7, cited from P. Bordewijk and H.L. Klaassen, *Wij laten ons niet kennen*, VNG uitgevers, The Hague, 2000, pp. 45–6 .

3 David Osborne and Peter Plastrik, *Banishing Bureaucracy*, Penguin, Reading, Massachusetts, 1997, p. 145.

4 Adapted from Henry Kissinger; J.A. de Bruijn, *Processen van verandering*, Lemma, Utrecht, 2000.

5 Hans Broere, *Symbol City*, Netherlands School of Public Administration (NSOB), The Hague, 2001.

6 For example in David Osborne and Peter Plastrik, *The Reinventor's Fieldbook. Tools for Transforming Your Government*, Jossey Bass, San Francisco, 2000, pp. 223ff.

7 David Osborne and Peter Plastrik, *Banishing Bureaucracy*, Penguin, Reading, Massachusetts, 1997.

8 David Osborne and Peter Plastrik, *Banishing Bureaucracy*, Penguin, Reading, Massachusetts, 1997, p. 145.

9 See for example Michael Quinn Patton, *Utilization-Focused Evaluation: The New Century Text*, Sage Publications, Thousand Oaks 1996. He presents the formula: 'Demand to produce outcome *minus* control about outcomes *plus* high stakes= corruption of indicators'.

10 See for example D. Coyle, *The Weightless World*, Capstone Publishing Ltd, Cambridge 1999, p. 23; R. Wigand, A., Picot and R. Reichwald, *Information*

Organization and Management: Expanding Markets and Corporate Boundaries, Wiley, Chichester, 1997.

11 Philippe D'Iribarne, *La logique de l'honneur – Gestion d'enterprises et traditions nationales*, Editions du Seuil, Paris, 1989.

12 David Osborne and Ted Gaebler, *Reinventing Government*, Penguin, Reading, Massachusetts, 1992.

13 The somewhat unfortunate Dutch translation used is 'technische functie'.

14 R.J. in 't Veld, *Relations between the State and Higher Education*, Kluwer Law International, The Hague 1996.

15 Andrea M. Serban and Joseph C. Burke, 'Meeting the performance challenge. a nine-state comparative analysis', *Public Productivity and Management Review* (1998), no. 2, pp. 157–77.

16 Aimee Franklin, 'Managing for results in Arizona, a fifth-year report card', *Public Productivity and Management Review* (1999), pp. 194–209, p. 205.

17 Aimee Franklin, 'Managing for results in Arizona, a fifth-year report card', *Public Productivity and Management Review* (1999), pp. 194–209, p. 205.

18 Cited from John F. Murray, *Intensive Care: A Doctor's Journal*, University of California Press, Los Angeles 2000. Murray describes the hierarchical relations and the course of the decision making processes in the Intensive Care Department. Many surgeons at the top of this hierarchy are less competent than their subordinates, but manage to maintain the hierarchical system. This matter-of-course position leads to the development of very strong egos and to the attitude represented in the quotation.

4 Design principles for performance measurement

1 Bobbi Low, Elinor Ostrom, Carl Simon and James Wilson, 'Redundancy and diversity in governing and managing common-pool resources', paper presented to the IASCP conference, Bloomington, Indiana, 2000.

2 Adapted from Michael Power, 'The Audit Explosion', in G. Mulgan (ed.), *Life after Politics*, Fontana Press, London, 1997, pp. 286-93. Similar categorizations can be found in, among other articles, Malcolm Smith *et al.*, 'Structure versus appraisal in the audit process: a test of Kinney's classification', *Managerial Auditing Journal* (2001), vol. 16, no. 1, pp. 40–9 (Smith discusses the distinction between structure and judgment); also: Lai Hong Chung *et al.*, 'The influence of subsidiary context and head office strategic management style on control of MNCs: the experience in Australia', *Accounting, Auditing and Accountability Journal* (2000), vol. 13, no. 5, pp. 647–68 (Chung discusses the distinction between output and behavioural control).

3 See for example Wim Veen, *Flexibel onderwijs voor nieuwe generaties studerenden*, Delft University of Technology, (DUT), Delft, 2001.

4 Hans de Bruijn and Claire de Nerée tot Babberich, *Opposites Attract, Competing Values in Knowledge Management*, Lemma, Utrecht, 2000.

5 Henry Mintzberg; *Structures in Fives: Designing Effective Organizations*, Prentice Hall, New Jersey, 1983.

6 Derived from Rein de Wilde, *De voorspellers. Een kritiek op de toekomstindustrie*, De Balie, Amsterdam, 2000, p. 128.

5 Trust and interaction

1 Haselbekke, A.G.J., H.L. Klaassen, A.P. Ros and R.J. in 't Veld, 'Counting

performance. Indicators as a tool for a (more) efficient management of decentralized governements' (in Dutch), VNG, The Hague, 1990.
2 See www.trouw.nl
3 J.A. de Bruijn, E.F. ten Heuvelhof and R.J. in 't Veld, *Process Management. Why Project Management Fails in Complex Decision Making Processes*, Kluwer Academic Publishers, Dordrecht, 2002.
4 David Osborne and Ted Gaebler, *Reinventing Government*, Penguin, Reading, Massachusetts, 1992, Appendix B.
5 *NRC Handelsblad*, 25 September 1996.
6 Delft University of Technology, *An Evaluation of the Use of the University Allocation Model 1996–1999*, Delft, 2000, p. 11 (in Dutch).

6   Content and variety

1 Lakoff, Robin T., *The Language War*, University of California Press, Berkeley, 2000.
2 Copied from planning and control details DJI, Ministry of Justice.
3 Lakoff, Robin T., *The Language War*, University of California Press, Berkeley 2000.
4 Geert Boeckaert and Ton Auwers, *Prestaties meten in de overheid*, Die Keure, Bruges, 1999.
5 Boje Larsen, 'One measurement is better than 1,000 opinions: is it?', *Managerial Auditing Journal* (2001), no. 2, pp. 63–8.
6 After P. Bordewijk and H.L Klaasen, *Don't Think You Can Measure Us*, VNG uitgevers, The Hague 2000, p. 45.
7 P. Bordewijk and H.L Klaasen, *Don't Think You Can Measure Us*, VNG uitgevers, The Hague 2000 p. 93.
8 P. Bordewijk and H.L Klaasen, *Don't Think You Can Measure Us*, VNG uitgevers, The Hague 2000.
9 P. Bordewijk and H.L Klaasen, *Don't Think You Can Measure Us*, VNG uitgevers, The Hague 2000.

7   Dynamic: towards lively performance measurement

1 Robert Quinn, *Beyond Rational Management*, Wiley, San Francisco, 1998.
2 William M. Rohe, Richard E. Adams, and Thomas A. Arcury, 'Community policing and planning', *Journal of the American Planning Assocation* (2001), vol. 67, no. 1.
3 J.A. de Bruijn and E.F. ten Heuvelhof, *Networks and Decision Making*, Lemma Publishers, Utrecht 2000.
4 J.A. de Bruijn and E.F. ten Heuvelhof, *Networks and Decision Making*, Lemma Publishers, Utrecht 2000.
5 J.A. de Bruijn and E.F. ten Heuvelhof, *Networks and Decision Making*, Lemma Publishers, Utrecht 2000.
6 R.J. in 't Veld, *Relations between the State and Higher Education*, Kluwer Law International, The Hague 1996.

8   The paradoxes of performance measurement

1 David Osborne and Peter Plastrik, *Banishing Bureaucracy*, Penguin, Reading, Massachusetts, 1997, p. 145.

Index